TAPESTRY

OF A LIFE

A MODERN ODYSSEY

SPANNING THREE CONTINENTS

NORA CURRAN

Dedication

To the memory of John Davison Curran

This is a labor of love dedicated to my grandchildren:

Charis, Noah, Nathan, Alexandria and Aimée.

When distance no longer matters!

Travel is fatal to prejudice, bigotry, and narrow-mindedness

Mark Twain

Table of Contents

PREFACE

The first edition of TAPESTRY OF A LIFE was launched in March 2020. I had several bookings and readings scheduled, but then Covid-19 upended everything with lockdowns and fear permeating every aspect of life. This new revised edition updates us with what has happened since. Five years may not seem long, but it can also bring momentous changes in one's life.

***

The man who came to London nearly twenty years ago, who got down on one knee and asked me to marry him—the man who brought me to America to be his wife, is no longer by my side.

John Davidson Curran passed away on Christmas Eve, 2023, after a long battle with COPD. I lost my companion, my rock, and my best friend. He has left a big void in my life. I feel his absence. We celebrated his life with a moving ceremony in February, where family and friends gathered to celebrate him. His was a life to be celebrated indeed. His daughter, Maellen, came from Albuquerque with her son Silas, and his sister Beth came from Massachusetts with her daughter Mary. Son Jonathan sent a moving video filled with loving memories. Many spoke, wrote, and mentioned the impact he had on their lives as a parent, colleague, and friend. Earlier, when he felt the end was near, Jadie had requested Silas to play taps at this funeral. A moving and fitting farewell to a veteran who served his country during the Korean War. It was also

Silas who played the Radames March from Aida as I walked up the aisle on a hot, sultry day, July 15, 2006, to marry Jadie.

Although he was born in California, Jadie grew up in New England. His accent betrayed him as a New Englander. He had many of the characteristics of that region – quiet, reserved, introverted. He was a man of few words, but every word counted. Not given to small talk or chit chat. We had a great deal in common, but in other ways, we were total opposites. I am a people person, gregarious, loquacious, and outgoing. John was not. They say opposites attract. We certainly felt an attraction for each other, and now that he's gone, my life is out of balance without him. My cousin's wife, a Massachusetts native, once said to me: "We New Englanders never talk or discuss feelings. That's not our thing." She could have been describing my husband in those words. He found it difficult to express emotions. While I was sorting out his stuff after he passed away, I was about to throw away some crumpled pieces of paper. Something, or someone, stopped me. Three small pieces of paper from a small notebook. I read it as tears flowed down my face. It was a letter from the grave—the words he could not say, but he could write down. He used to say, "I let my fingers do the talking," meaning his typing. We used to joke that it was a good thing we had met in the email age because his handwriting was terrible. "You should have been a doctor," I once to him.

This was his handwritten farewell to me:

Last Sunday in Feb. 2023

Dearest Nora,

I've spent the last few years of my life thinking about the matchless depth you brought to it and the unique joy you bring to all fortunate to know you. There is no way I could ever repay you for your loving strength or the unique character you shared with me. In the end, I have the comfort that perhaps I also contributed to that strength in my own small way, and I trust that you will take the depth of our life, hoping it will help others to do the same.

I love you to the end, even beyond our physical love, to a new relationship now etched in eternity.

As you so often say to friends "I love you and leave you." This time it's forever. God bless.

Love, Jadie

He never said it to me, but he wrote it down, and I'm glad I found it. I shall always treasure it.

***

Trying to make sense of a life before presenting it to the outside world is a challenge. There are choices to be made—selection, simplification, elaboration, and admission.

Perhaps "tapestry" is not the right word to describe my life. I know how much planning and preparation goes into weaving a tapestry. Thought has to be given to the warp, the weft, the different yarns and threads, the colors, and the design. The threads of my life—interwoven and meshed—form the fabric of my history. Trying to choose the right word, the "bon mot," is like choosing that special color, fabric, or highlight to weave through the warp. If only life could be planned as carefully. Most of my tapestries are free-form. I work with no fixed plan, and serendipitously, the shapes and colors come together—just like the various pieces of one's life come together, often haphazardly, to form a whole. *Patchwork* might be a better word. I have a patchwork skirt. It hangs loose and is very comfortable. I've had it for a long time. Looking at it closely, I can see that the trapezoid patches are carelessly put together—some colors clash. The patterns on some pieces are not pretty, and some pieces have faded. But somehow, seen as a whole, they manage to make an interesting piece of cloth. The underside, however, is rather messy with fraying threads. Life can be like that—a patchwork. Memories of places, people, events, and hopes are patched together, sometimes loosely and sometimes tightly. We don't mind showing the 'good' side but prefer to hide the underside. A memoir should show both sides—that's honest writing.

The front cover is a picture of the ocean with a surfer. It symbolizes the ocean as a unifier. It connects continents, it welcomes rivers, and it reflects the color and mood of the sky. The moon controls its tides. It has moods—from turbulent anger to quiet calm movement, it spouts jetsam and flotsam and takes it back again. Life is like the ocean—we surf along with its ups and downs, sometimes riding on the crest of a wave, and sometimes alongside it. At other times, we can be thrown off balance when life throws us those curve balls. But we must persist. Get back again on the surfboard and ride into the unknown.

A subtitle to my story could be *On the Other Hand* because when confronted with an unfamiliar situation, behavior, culture or tradition, I try to see both sides—mine and theirs. Not that I enjoy the murky gray between black and white, but in many cases, there are no absolutes. Even when I hold strong views, I can still see the viewpoint of others without changing mine. This is what makes human interactions both special and tricky.

Writing a memoir is simply writing about oneself—people you have known, events in your life that left their mark, relationships, places, and how you experienced them, both then and now— through the prism of time and hindsight. It's as if you were disrobing in front of your readers. You are exposing a body of work with its scars, bruises, warts, and all. It takes courage to open up one's life to the outside world. It can be challenging because sometimes, you have to take out a few skeletons, which have been deliberately locked up in closets, and show them to the public.

At times, I hesitated to write about certain events and individuals as I grappled with ethical questions such as: *Can I really tell that story? Would it hurt people I know and love or damage my relationship with them? Is it too shocking?* I think every memoirist has had to deal with these issues.

I have tried to put together those pieces that I think are interesting, informative, and entertaining. As I look back over several decades, I realize that my perceptions and perspectives have changed. I have tried to be honest and forthright. I hope this comes through. A few names have been changed to protect the privacy of certain individuals.

Some readers may be upset or offended by my honesty. However, this is *my* memoir, my experiences, impressions, and reactions seen through *my* eyes.

I have often asked myself the reasons for writing my story. Someone once said that writing a memoir is therapeutic. This memoir is not an attempt at catharsis or laying down ghosts. It began when my eldest granddaughter, Charis, asked me about her antecedents. Her inquiry made me open the chambers of my memory, and the stories just started tumbling out. I began writing. Once the memory dyke was breached, there was no stopping the flow. I surprised myself because I had heard so much about "writer's block" and "fear of the blank page." To my relief, that was not the case.

I write because I enjoy it, along with the chuckles I get looking back on events and people who are part of this tapestry. So I plead *mea culpa*, not to expiate my sin, but to share the chuckles. So please fasten your seatbelts and enjoy the flight. I promise you a smooth landing.

Nora Curran

La Mesa, California

INTRODUCTION

I am the daughter of a father who once said to me, "Education is wasted on a woman."

Those cataclysmic words propelled me to prove him wrong. Our relationship became a battle of wills, and I was determined to win. He had money and power on his side. I had only my wits.

It is ironic that a father whose bookshelves held the works of Goethe, Dostoyevsky, Shakespeare, and Victor Hugo believed that education was wasted on a woman. Did he consider educated women a threat? Did he believe a college education would diminish his control over me? He was willing to pay for expensive private schools, but after high school, as college loomed on the horizon, he decided it was time for me to return "home." His home. A home I had managed to escape briefly when he sent me to boarding school in England.

From a young age, I somehow knew—almost instinctively—that education would be my key to freedom, an escape from a dysfunctional parent. The male-dominated society of the Greek island where I was born, aided and abetted by the teachings of the Greek Orthodox Church, primed girls to be respectful and compliant. Gender roles were clearly defined between them and us—*them* being the dominant males, and *us* the subservient females.

Those words—*Education is wasted on a woman*—fanned the spark of independence in me into an inferno, and it continues to burn.

This is my story—how I managed to break free and soar above those constraints. My flight took me from Cyprus to England, Hong Kong, Mongolia, China, and finally to the United States.

My education began when I realized I had choices—that I could take risks and live with the consequences. And it is ongoing. I remain a perennial student, a work in progress. I want to keep learning. Some lessons are painful, but perhaps those are the ones that teach us the most.

Education is never wasted on anyone—be it man or woman.

CHAPTER ONE

ONCE UPON A TIME

I have the dubious honor—or dishonor—of being a bastard. On the Greek island of Cyprus, where I was born, unwed couples living together, like my parents, were ostracised by society. The islanders held firm ideas of right and wrong. The Greek Orthodox Church determined moral propriety. "Bastard" was an unwelcome label back in the dark ages of the 1940s. Those born out of wedlock were branded with the stigma of illegitimacy. I was branded, all right. The branding was on my heart.

Illegitimacy, as old as humankind, has spawned swear words and colorful euphemisms. In England, a bastard child was said to be born on the wrong side of the sheets. What's the right side, anyway?

My parents lived their shame openly, referring to each other as husband and wife. But everyone on the island knew there had never been a wedding. Since my parents refused to live under the radar, I had a normal childhood. I was not kept hidden or secret. Mum encouraged me in the arts—piano and ballet lessons. Dad encouraged me to read the classics and paid for my tuition and private schools.

Most of my parents' circle of friends were Brits and other foreign nationals. From a young age, growing up in a polyglot environment, I learned to speak several languages. It was a Romanian friend who first called me Norika, which became my nickname. Mum always called me

Norika, even though I was christened Eleonora, after my paternal grandmother.

I was eight years old when I found out I was illegitimate. My mum, Galathea, had disappeared for twenty-four hours. Alex, my father, refused to tell me where she had gone. The following day, he took me to a friend's house, and Mum was there. She hugged me tightly and, between sobs, told me she had left because Dad refused to marry her. At the time, I did not quite understand the enormity of that, but I was glad to have her back home with us.

I think it was at that moment that my relationship with my father underwent a subtle change. My perception of him was that he made Mum sad by not giving her what she wanted.

After that, life resumed its usual rhythm—Mum cried, Dad shouted and slammed doors, and the cat tried to get out of the way. I envied the cat when he managed to escape.

In between the rows, there were peaceful times. I think my Dad personified the term "control freak." He traveled extensively overseas on business and sometimes took me along. Mum stayed behind. On his return, she had to account for every penny, as he went over the books with a fine-tooth comb, questioning everything. It was his way of maintaining control, along with frequent outbursts of rage. He could create a scene at the drop of a hat, anywhere, anytime—even outside the home.

I vividly remember one such incident. We were visiting London and staying in a hotel just off Piccadilly Circus. As we were having a meal in the hotel dining room, Dad picked up a fork and stared at it. He held it at arm's length and kept bringing it closer to him. Back and forth. I watched him, mesmerized.

"It's filthy," he muttered. "Can't you see?" I wasn't sure whether he was speaking to me or the people around us. He then summoned the waiter and unleashed his unrighteous indignation on him.

"What's this?" he asked. The waiter had no idea.

"Here, take a look." The waiter looked nonplussed. Then Dad shoved the fork under the waiter's nose, saying at the top of his voice, "Can't you see? Are you blind or what? This is filthy!"

Now we had an audience—the entire dining room. The waiter suggested that perhaps the dishwasher had simply missed that fork. Wrong answer! My Dad expected the waiter to squirm, apologize, and bring a clean fork. "Get me the manager!" he demanded.

When the manager arrived, Dad continued his tirade.

"I have traveled all over the world and have never, ever, seen such filthy cutlery. What is this? You can give us food poisoning. Who checks the cleanliness of the silverware that comes out of the dishwasher?"

I don't remember how that episode ended, but I remember my embarrassment and humiliation. It was one of many scenes Dad caused with his apoplectic outbursts.

Domestic rows were equally violent. Usually, my parents waited until I was asleep or in school. They were not confined to shouting and slamming doors. He also used his fists, and even a strap, on Mum. At times, I was so worried I begged her to leave, fearing for her life. But when the rows subsided, I begged her to stay and not leave me.

"If I could take you with me, I would leave," she told me, "but I have nowhere to go."

As his business prospered, Dad was able to have a house built on a piece of land he had bought. Our new home was fairly close to my elementary school, and I could hear the school bell. I was often late for morning class. I guess the dysfunction at home had something to do with it. I was too young to work out the reasons. But I do recall the teacher telling me that if I were late again, I had to bring a note from my parents. Soon after this stern warning, I was late again. When I saw my classroom door closed and the lesson had already started, I turned back to get a note from my parents.

As I opened our front gate, I saw my mum jump from the first-floor bedroom window and fall onto the tiled veranda, her knees bruised and bloodied. She was trying to escape Dad's blows. It was not the first—nor the last—time she was bruised from his beatings.

"You mustn't tell anyone," she'd say. "No one must know."

Often, she explained a black eye or visible bruise as: "I just bumped into the doorpost," or, "I fell off my bicycle." Did anyone believe her? I don't know.

Despite the rows and beatings, she refused to become a victim. She had made her choice and had to live with it. To the outside world, she put on a brave face. She displayed a vitality and energy that the more uptight matrons of that time might have envied. Dad was never able to extinguish that spark in her.

In her way, she found ways to get around my father's bullying. My dad had forbidden her to take me to church or visit her family. She insisted that churchgoing could not be ruled out. For Greeks, there is no separation between Church and State. If you are born Greek, you are automatically Greek Orthodox. Babies are christened by total immersion and given a biblical name. I asked her one day, "How come your name is not in the Bible or the name of one of the saints?"

"Ah... My name is Galathea. It's from Greek mythology. Greek mythology, and all the stories about our ancestors, are like a second religion to us. The Church turns a blind eye when a name from the Ancients is chosen."

"So I could have been named Clytemnestra?"

"Of course. Or Iphigenia."

"How come I was christened Eleonora?" I asked.

"That's another story. I'll tell you what happened. You were growing up, and your father refused to have you christened. He kept making excuses, saying it wasn't necessary, or that you would catch cold, or that the priest would drop you as he anointed you with olive oil."

Olive oil is a panacea for Greeks. Not only is it used in cooking and salad dressings, we use it in poultices, rub it into our hair, all over our bodies for aches and pains, and anything else you can think of. My parents kept a demijohn of olive oil in our kitchen.

During a baptism, the priest uses copious amounts of olive oil to anoint the infant. My dad used that as a pretext, claiming the priest would drop me as I slipped out of his oily grip. Mum, however, continued to plead, and eventually, he caved in.

"We set the date and went to the big cathedral in Nicosia. The priest asked your dad what name he'd chosen for you, and he proudly announced: 'Victoria Eleonora.' The priest balked. 'What kind of names are these?' he asked. 'I can't accept them. They're not Greek names.'" Mum continued.

"The priest was rude, and your father responded in his usual way—with rage, cursing the priest and shouting: 'I never wanted her done in the first place. You can keep your filthy hands off my baby!' And with that, he grabbed you and stormed out."

I could almost visualize the scene—Dad stomping out and leaving everyone standing there, gaping. He hated priests.

"I was fraught," Mum said. "I knew this was the only chance you had of being a Christian." In the Greek Church, if you are not baptized, you're not considered a Christian.

"So I begged the priest to relent and give in. He saw that your father was serious about not getting you 'done'. Eventually, there was a 'deal'. The priest said he would accept only one 'heathen' name. So we dropped the Victoria and you were christened Eleonora, which is your paternal grandma's name."

And that's how I became Eleonora. I don't think Clytemnestra would have suited me.

***

For a woman of her generation, it took spunk and rebelliousness on Mum's part to leave her parental home at the age of sixteen and run away with my dad, who was twice her age and already married. It caused quite a scandal at the time. It also disgraced her family. Families with no money—the poor—possessed only one thing of value: their reputation. A good name was like money in the bank. Even better.

Years later, Mum's younger sister, my Aunt Mary, recounted the story to me. "Our parents were simple village folk. They went to the capital, Nicosia, to find work. Dad was a shopkeeper, and initially, the business prospered. They had six children, two boys and four girls, but only the girls survived."

Aunt Mary explained that although illiterate, my grandmother valued education. For a short while, they had a servant, Anna, and Grandmother sent her to school also, together with her daughters—not always with a happy consequence, as some of the school staff and pupils treated Anna with open disdain. Servants were not meant to be educated. They were poor village women, like my grandmother, brought to the city to work in rich households.

After my grandfather lost his business, the family suffered great hardship.

"In order to support us, your grandfather took a job in the asbestos mines, away from home. Mother had to take in lodgers to make ends meet. She'd go to the grocery store and beg for credit. Worst of all, our parents could not afford a dowry," Aunt Mary recalled.

Back then, a woman could not marry without a dowry. The burden of providing for daughters was a millstone around the neck of poor households. The minute a girl was born, the parents would start a hope chest. It was also the tradition for brothers to go to work, before they married themselves, to provide for their sisters' dowries. It was considered bad form for a brother to marry before his unwed sisters.

Growing up, I often heard my dad boast that my dowry was a sure thing. "Nora will have everything one day. She has a secure future. Nothing to worry about," he bragged. I can't help but smile now at the irony of those words, and how differently things turned out.

Mum and her three sisters had other ideas for themselves, considered risqué and unconventional at the time. You were not meant to have aspirations above your social status. Women were supposed to live at home, get married, and have babies—enabling men to rule the roost. It was very much a male-dominated society.

With help from a kind relative, my mother got a place at the most prestigious secondary school in Nicosia, a Gymnasium, which is like a Grammar School.

Mum often told me, with some pride, that she was only one of four girls admitted to the Gymnasium. But she never told me the full story:

that she was expelled and never finished her studies. I learned the alternate truth from Aunt Mary, many years later.

At the time, there was no official supplier of school uniforms for female students. They were simply told the type and color of the clothes required—blue. But Mum had her own ideas. According to Aunt Mary: "Galathea was a very pretty, vivacious girl with bright blue eyes and a good figure. The color she chose for her school uniform was a much brighter blue than the school stipulated. It emphasized the brightness of her eyes, and the cut of the clothes made her much too attractive to the boys. The school told her that she must replace her uniform with cloth of a more sober color. She rebelled and said that her family was poor and she could not afford to do so. When, after some time, she still refused to comply, the school authorities asked her to leave. She did not attend any other school after that."

That's how I learned that my mum was a high school dropout.

I often wondered why someone so beautiful would end up with a man like my dad. I think, apart from her desire to be independent, she feared that she would meet the same fate as her older sister Alecca, who was forced into an arranged marriage.

Alecca was considered the most beautiful of the four sisters. Good looks would get you into trouble, but not into wedlock. A dowry was the most essential inducement for marriage. Virginity was highly valued and expected of a woman. A girl had to be *virgo intacta* until her wedding night. And proof of the fact was demanded. There had to be a showing.

According to the custom of the day, especially in the countryside, the morning after the consummation of the marriage, the mother-in-law would hang the bloodied sheet over the balcony, for all to see. This was the showing and proof that the girl had been a virgin, and the boy had done his duty as a man. The couple was left in no doubt of what was expected of them. The honor and reputation of two families was at stake. If it came out that the girl was not "intact" or could not prove her virginity, it could be grounds for annulment.

The mores and traditions of that period left me baffled and angry. It was yet another demonstration of how the Church and men held sway over women, reducing them to chattels—traded for dowries, with a price placed on their virginity.

***

In the Middle Ages, virginity was a sought-after commodity, primarily because it was the surest way to guarantee paternity. Heaven forbid that someone else's child—a bastard—might inherit. That's why a 'soiled' woman could never get married. Not only did the Church demand that women be chaste and pure—the rich and powerful also needed it to guarantee the continuation of their lineage through breeding.

Fast forward to 1981—not the Middle Ages—when the British royal family was looking for a suitable bride for Prince Charles, who definitely was not a virgin by the time he married Diana. The British press wrote that the future bride had to be a virgin. Several of his girlfriends were eliminated because they had a certain reputation.

***

No wonder Mum wanted to escape. She must have felt suffocated by this blind observance of tradition. But I also realized the enormity of what she had done, and how her actions and behavior had brought shame on her family. The poor were expected to conform. Rebellion and eccentricity were the privilege of the rich and powerful. She had broken all the sacred taboos of the time.

So how did they force Aunt Alecca to marry Uncle Andreas? I wondered. Once again, I delved into Aunt Mary's memory reservoir.

"We were destitute. When Andreas offered to marry Alecca, my parents were over the moon. To them, it was a miracle," Mary recalled.

"Woe betide any young man who approached a single lady without a chaperone. In those days, matchmakers were indispensable. Usually, an older relative, or even a professional matchmaker, came to the house to plead the young man's case."

How strange that the wooing was done through go-betweens. For some reason, the whole idea smacked of another way of controlling women—especially those from poor households. The matchmaker extolled Andreas' qualities: he was hardworking, had a good and steady job as an elementary school teacher, and once he passed his English exams, he would get a better-paid job in a government-funded school.

To the parents' consternation, Alecca refused to marry Andreas. In those days, girls did not have much say in these arranged marriages. She was defying her parents and convention.

Alecca had already spent some time on the Greek mainland and studied poultry farming in Athens for a couple of years until the money ran out. In Athens, she experienced a different lifestyle and a new freedom. It was very much a case of: "You don't go back to the farm after you've seen Paree." Unfortunately, she had to return to the "farm" and never realized her dreams.

My grandmother, aware that there would never be another opportunity like this, locked her up in her room. For three days, Alecca had no food or water—until she relented and agreed to marry Andreas.

I remember Uncle Andreas. He was a rough diamond: kind, good-looking, and loud. He had a booming voice and spoke with the dialect and heavy accent of village folk.

My grandmother's health was beginning to fail. It's possible that she sensed she did not have long to live. She wanted to see at least one daughter married before she closed her eyes. The marriage contract was drawn up, witnessed by the priest, signed and sealed. If the engagement was ever broken, the girl was considered "soiled." Sometimes, engagements lasted several years, until the couple had sufficient money to marry.

A few years later, another daughter, Nikki, was betrothed, and when her fiancé broke off the engagement, she sued him for breach of contract and received the princely sum of £200. She used the money to study nursing.

In 1935, my grandmother died. Andreas and Alecca moved in with my grandfather and his other three daughters. One down, three more to go—all of them without dowries.

***

My father, Alex, started coming to the house since he and Andreas did some work together. The visits were initially for business—and then for my mother, Galathea. They fell in love, and on the day she turned sixteen, she ran off with him. This caused quite a stir on the island—a scandal and a shame. Aunt Mary told me that Dad's wife and family laid siege to my grandparents' home. For days, they stood outside shouting and hurling insults. Young Mary was terrified, as she could not leave the house.

Despite assurances that once he got divorced, he would marry her, Dad never made good on his promise. He claimed that his wife would demand too much alimony.

After the honeymoon period, a few years later, and once he started to mistreat her, Mum returned to her father's house. By then, Aunt Mary had a good job. She offered to pay for my mother to get some kind of training that would enable her to be independent. Since Mum was now considered a soiled woman, marriage was out of the question. She was now branded—but unlike my branding, hers was self-inflicted.

Before she could avail herself of Mary's offer, Dad feigned sickness. He called for her from his "deathbed." She went to see him. I guess they kissed and made up, and soon after, I was conceived. There was no escape for her now. She had to make the best of her situation.

If it weren't for his tight fists—both on the purse and on her—I think they could have been happy, but it was not to be.

***

My father lived to be a hundred. He was born in 1903 and died in 2004. He lived through two world wars, the arrival of the motor car, the airplane, the telephone, and the computer. He was a Renaissance man and self-made. He could speak nine languages and could quote Goethe in German, Shakespeare in English, Dante in Italian, and Cervantes in Spanish. He also spoke Turkish and read Arabic. He could hold court and entertain a room full of people.

He could also be mean, sadistic, and unforgiving. Growing up as a little girl, I knew only the good side—until things changed.

My dad's mother, Victoria Eleonora, was a Sephardic Jew from Constantinople—better known as Istanbul today. It hosted a large community of Jews. Most of them had fled the Spanish Inquisition in the 15th century and the subsequent pogroms in Europe and found shelter there. The reigning Sultan realized that he could make use of their education and expertise. He offered them a home and religious freedom, so long as they were loyal to him. They became his astronomers, mathematicians, mapmakers, physicians, and administrators. At one point, Jews made up ten percent of Constantinople's population. However, over the centuries, as the power of the Ottoman Empire waned, they lost their privileged status and lived as one of the many oppressed ethnic groups under the Turks.

Towards the end of the 19th and early 20th century, Victoria Eleonora left Turkey and went to Cyprus. It's possible she sensed the rise of Turkish nationalism and feared that pogroms would start again. I think Jews have a sixth sense when persecutions are about to resume.

Cyprus was then a British Protectorate, and my grandmother felt safe there. A few years later, she brought her younger sister, Rachel, to join her. Victoria Eleonora made her living by singing in upscale nightclubs. She sang songs in Spanish, Greek, Turkish, and Ladino. At home, they spoke Ladino—an amalgam of Old Spanish, Hebrew, Aramaic, and some Portuguese. It also carried influences from Ottoman Turkish, Levantine Arabic, Greek, and Bulgarian. No wonder my father was such an amazing linguist.

Dad told me that his mother converted to the Greek Orthodox religion in order to marry her impresario—a Greek from Smyrna. They had two sons, my father and his younger brother, my Uncle Nick. The impresario soon abandoned them, and my grandmother struggled to raise the boys on her own. Whenever I asked my dad about his father, his color changed to purple. He hated him with a passion.

Victoria Eleonora had a heart condition. She died when my dad was in his early teens, and his brother, my Uncle Nick, around nine or so. On her deathbed, she made my father promise that he'd take care of his younger brother.

Dad was not forthcoming about his upbringing or his early days. He would occasionally mention snippets, but I could never get the full picture.

I am grateful to my Aunt Mary, once again, for this apocryphal story. The night my grandmother Victoria Eleonora died, the two orphan boys went to the priest to ask him to bury her. He asked for money. The boys had no money to grease his palm. They returned home, found a handcart, placed their mother's corpse in it, and carried her to the cemetery. Under cover of darkness, they found a newly dug grave and dumped her there. No wonder my dad hated priests and religion. Years later, I would joke that he was "a born-again atheist," but now I understand why.

A Greek family took in the two orphan boys. They had a sickly daughter and told my dad that if he married her, they would see to his brother's education. My father agreed, honoring the promise he made to his mother on her deathbed. This was the wife he was to abandon years later for my mother.

***

Despite his humble beginnings, my father became prominent in the radical and liberal movements of the time. He was instrumental in setting up the first trade unions on the island. But he soon became disillusioned with politics and concentrated on his business. He kept abreast of world events and current affairs by reading and listening to the BBC World Service. Most evenings, we'd turn on the old Bakelite radio, and after a few minutes—waiting for it to warm up—we heard the clipped tones of the announcer saying: "This is London calling," followed by Big Ben and then the *Lilliburlero* tune.

When it came to politics, Dad was cynical—and often right. "It's all about money and power," he said. "Those at the top only care for one thing: how to stay on top. And they don't care about anything or anyone else."

Dad had a lot of firsts to his credit: he imported the first car to Cyprus, as well as the first washing machine and refrigerator. Every year, we had a new washing machine. Mum would invite all her female friends to give them a demo of the new machine.

Back then, houses were not built with plumbing to accommodate these new-fangled contraptions. The washing machine had to be placed next to the kitchen sink, with a hose attached to the faucet, while another hose was hooked over the sink for the dirty water to empty. During one of these demos, the vigor of the spin cycle unlocked the wheels. The two hoses fell to the ground, gushing water on everything and everyone while the machine continued waltzing around the wet kitchen floor.

***

Every year, around Greek Easter time, a grateful customer brought us a lamb that was tethered in our backyard. Oh, how I loved playing with my new pet. I spent hours talking to him and hugging his soft fleece—but then he would vanish. After a few years, I realized that the meat on my plate was my pet. I could not eat any meat after that.

"What's wrong with you? Eat your food," my parents scolded. If Dad left the room, I surreptitiously fed our dog, Toby, who sat under the table, patiently waiting.

My parents kept saying: "You don't know how lucky you are to have food on your plate. Eat up! Think of all the starving children in Africa." To which I would reply, "Then please, give it to them."

My father was the wholesale meat supplier for the British forces in Cyprus, so vegetarianism was not an option in our home.

***

I was a voracious reader. As an only child, books were my companions. I looked forward to getting *Classics Illustrated*. It was a weekly or monthly publication (I can't remember the frequency), and I could not wait to read the next story. I particularly loved Dickens' *Oliver Twist*, *Great Expectations*, and *A Christmas Carol*, as well as stories by Hans Christian Andersen and Jane Austen.

Dad was also a good storyteller. He recounted stories from Greek mythology, and I loved hearing about Jason and the Argonauts, the heroes of the *Iliad*, and the travels of Odysseus.

"Dad, why is it that Greeks were always killing each other and the stories are so gory?"

"That's because people are nasty and do terrible things to each other."

"Even in families? Like Agamemnon sacrificing his own daughter and then his wife had to kill him?"

"Yes, those are the Greek tragedies."

"You and Mum fight a lot. Is that a Greek tragedy?"

He laughed. "Perhaps," he said.

"Are you going to kill each other also?"

"I don't know about that, but families have their problems and rows. The people who can hurt you most are those from your own family."

"Then who can you trust?"

"No one."

"Not even you, Dad?"

"Not even me."

Those words were to prove prophetic in the years to come.

***

His treatment of Galathea was eventually too much for her. When I was eleven, they separated. I woke up one morning and she was gone. My father told me never to mention her name again. He forbade me to see her or have anything to do with her. This was hard for an eleven-year-old child. If he found out that my mum had sneaked into the schoolyard during recess just to speak to me, he would beat me. That's when he changed from a loving Dad to a child beater. My mum was no longer at the receiving end of his rage, so now the blows fell on me.

The beatings were always because of a few "secret" meetings I had with Mum—in the schoolyard, in the street outside, or at a friend's house. He would terrorize me by barking, "You've seen her, haven't you?"

"No. Who, Dad?"

"Don't play games with me. That woman. I told you not to have anything to do with her. You're lying. I told you not to see that woman—you disobeyed me."

Terrified, I denied it, and of course, I knew what was coming. The beatings were fierce. I often went to school with welts on my legs where he had beaten me with a strap, a coat hanger, or his fists.

During those years, the stigma of illegitimacy haunted me. I felt ashamed and soiled. An eleven-year-old girl on a small island—where men often beat women and no one raised an eyebrow—had to suffer in silence. There was no Me Too movement. It was very much a man's world.

It was not the kind of childhood I would have chosen. I imagined that I was adopted. That my real parents would turn up and claim me. Or that a rich uncle from America would come and take me away.

At the time, I did not know about my mother's failure to continue her secondary education. But somehow, instinctively, I knew that *education* was the key that could open the door to freedom. I craved to be away—somewhere safe, without shouting, without all that rage, put-downs, beatings, and crying. I knew I had to get away, and that the only way out was through education. I also realized that the way my mother—and many other women of her generation—sought to escape poverty by looking for a male savior, husband, or lover, was not the answer. The woman would still not be free, since without any financial independence, she would be entirely dependent on the male provider.

To outsiders, I appeared to have a privileged childhood. I often accompanied my father on trips to Europe or to visit relatives in Israel. He took me to the opera at La Scala in Milan, to Covent Garden and the Royal Ballet in London. I saw a beautiful ballet performance on the shores of Lake Maggiore and Lake Constance, and I spent a summer studying German at the University of Vienna. Dad loved opera, Viennese operettas, and classical music. He instilled in me a love for this kind of music. We had a wind-up gramophone and played classical music on those old, scratchy 78 rpm records.

Inside, however, I was still an eleven-year-old aching and longing for her mum. Trips to Europe could not remove the sadness and pain. I had one good friend, Miranda, and after school we went to her house and did our homework together. She had a normal family, and they included and welcomed me into their home. Most nights, I cried myself to sleep.

In his mind, Dad thought he was being a good father. The truth is, he never had a role model, so he had no idea how a father should act or raise a daughter. Never having had a father, he did not know how to be one.

Dad had come a long way from the day he had to carry his mother's dead body in a handcart and dump her into an empty grave. But I believe the hardships he endured warped him and hardened him.

After Mum's departure, Dad sent me to a French convent boarding school. This was in another town, not in Nicosia. I guess he thought he could put distance between me and my mother. He wanted me to learn French and to continue my Greek and English lessons. I was always top of my class. When I took my matriculation in French, I came first in the entire island. My father announced it in the local newspaper. But to me, he simply said, "I guess the exam must have been easy."

He never praised me for anything. He thought that criticism and put-downs would make me work harder.

The kind nuns became my surrogate mothers. If I was not reading or studying, I often found refuge in the cool of the chapel. I sat there looking at the statues and talking to God. I told Him all my problems and asked Him to bring my parents back together. I felt God was listening to me. In teaching us to pray, the nuns explained that it was simply a matter of just speaking to God. And so I did. I would pour out my heart to Him and feel a peace descend on me. The chapel was my refuge.

I continued to study hard. But things were about to change. The Greek Cypriots were becoming restless under British colonial rule. One night, loud explosions woke up our entire dormitory of girls. The independence movement had begun. There was a lot of fear and excitement in the room. The nuns tried to calm us. As we were scrambling back into our beds, I said, "Why didn't they wait until the morning to explode their bombs?"

Lilian, the girl whose bed was next to mine, hissed, "Bastard!" I pretended not to hear her. But it hurt.

***

A combination of events led to my leaving Cyprus: the war of independence, my father's alarm at what he perceived to be my increased religiosity, and his current love interest—a Viennese lady, Luise—who later became my stepmother—decided my fate.

"It's no longer safe around here. This war will go on for a while. I've decided to find you a school in England," Dad said.

"But Dad, I think Mère Marc wants me to go to France for my studies."

"Yup, another convent school. You've had enough of convent education. I think England is better for you. Besides, you have a British passport, and it's easier to go to England."

I knew he wanted to remove me from the influence of nuns. He felt they were brainwashing me with religion. He thought England was a sufficiently atheist country and that, away from the influence of nuns, I would leave all that "religious nonsense" behind.

In 1959, I left Cyprus for England. I was both excited and apprehensive—filled with anticipation and hesitation. What would my new school be like? Who would be my new classmates? I knew I would miss the kind nuns and the friends I was leaving behind. As the plane took off, I looked down and saw my small island disappear under the clouds. I was now headed for a much bigger island. From the familiar to the unknown. It was a bittersweet moment. A parting of the ways.

CHAPTER TWO

BREAKING FREE

My English boarding school was in Ascot, home of the famous horse races. During Ascot Week, when the whole world seemed to descend upon our otherwise quiet, rural surroundings, we were not allowed out and were virtually grounded. Apart from that one week, we were allowed to go for walks in the beautiful English countryside and even ride our bicycles in Windsor Forest. When the royal family was in residence at the castle, we sometimes caught a glimpse of them driving by. I once saw the Queen, wearing a headscarf, driving her Range Rover. Having thought of her as always wearing a crown or a tiara, I felt cheated and disappointed. Seeing her with a headscarf was not what I had imagined.

I was not used to the British climate. I could never get warm enough and hugged the radiators every chance I had. I looked forward to a mug of hot cocoa during elevenses. Aside from swimming and tennis, I was not keen on sports. I thought the sports teacher was cruel for making us go out in wet and freezing conditions. Sport was part of the curriculum, and not optional.

It was a rich girls' school, and my father frequently reminded me how much it was costing him. He sent me the monthly bills and asked me to check and make sure he was not being overcharged. I felt humiliated—and guilty—for some reason as if I were responsible for all this expense. Children often blame themselves when confronted by an abusive parent. This was my father's duality: he boasted of sending me to one of the most expensive schools in England and then complained about the cost of tennis or piano lessons.

During my last two years in school, the Profumo scandal—which eventually brought down the Macmillan government—was in full swing. We pored over the newspapers, reading all the gory details about affairs between peers of the realm and call girls. I discovered that *The Daily Telegraph* had the best information, as it provided full transcripts of the court proceedings. Perhaps that's when my interest in politics and current affairs began.

Someone had also smuggled in an unexpurgated copy of *Lady Chatterley's Lover* by D.H. Lawrence—considered risqué at the time because the book had been banned for obscenity. We hid it under our bed covers and read it, after lights out, with a flashlight, looking for the naughty words that had caused it to be banned.

Aware that a good education was my key to freedom, I committed to studying hard and getting good grades. While my classmates enjoyed playing lacrosse, netball, and tennis, I buried myself in the library to read and do homework. The girls teased me and called me a "bluestocking," but I didn't care.

Like most teenage girls about to be launched into society, my peers talked about their coming-out dances as debutantes. They gossiped about who would attend and which suitable boys their mothers would invite to their balls. Their parents wanted to ensure their daughters were matched with boys from the right background with good prospects. I realized that these parents had the same hopes and aspirations for their offspring that my grandparents had for their daughters—only their tactics were different.

Our headmistress, Miss Wickham, wore thick-rimmed glasses and looked fierce most of the time. At my father's request, I took private German lessons with her. To her credit, she tried to widen our horizons and raise the aspirations of both the girls and their parents. She collected some highly qualified and energetic teachers who encouraged us to consider college instead of secretarial school or a career in nursing. They urged us to think big: "Why be a nurse, when you can be a doctor?" or "Why be a secretary when you can be a CEO or manager?"

My favorite subject was history, for which I credit Miss Asher, our history teacher. She inspired us to study the cause and effect of historical events such as the Renaissance, the French Revolution, and the English Civil War. She had an encyclopaedic knowledge—not only of history, but also of writers, philosophers, and politics. She introduced me to 18th- and 19th-century thinkers and encouraged us to ask questions and reason out the answers. I joined the debating society and loved the freedom to expound ideas, discuss, and argue points of view.

I was maturing—not only physically, but also mentally and emotionally. By studying the Age of Enlightenment, I felt I was achieving my own enlightenment. I too had choices—or so I thought. I had no idea that a nightmare lurked around the corner.

I dreaded leaving school, knowing what would come. There would be no coming-out ball for me. I so badly wanted to go to college and keep on learning. That's when my father dropped his devastating bombshell by declaring: "Education is wasted on a woman!"

"But Dad, I worked so hard! I have good grades. I want to go to university."

"No. You'll come back to Cyprus and marry... someone who'll help me in my business. In the meantime, you can lend a hand."

I felt betrayed and helpless. I argued I pleaded, I begged. Looking back, with the advantage of 20/20 hindsight, I think he also feared that a college education would empower me, and that I'd become independent of him—his male hegemony was threatened. He'd lose control.

I had no money and no advocates. If I returned to Cyprus, I'd be trapped, and I also feared that the beatings and humiliations would resume. I had no intention of being peddled on the marriage circuit, for young men to come along sniffing at my dad's bank account and monetary worth. A rich dad meant a good, handsome dowry to go with my hand in marriage. Yikes!

Dad was good at giving mixed messages. His attitude toward women was antediluvian. For him, there were only two kinds of women—those you bedded, and the ones in your family who were beyond the pale; that is, beyond the reach of other predators.

I was a fledgling ready to leave the nest, but my wings were being clipped. My mind was sending out SOS messages—to where? Where could I turn? I needed a lifeline, and quickly. It came with an idea:

"Dad, if you want me to come and assist you in your business, I need to learn something about commerce. How about going to a business school for a year to get the skills I need?"

To my surprise, he agreed. To his credit, he found the best business school in London—Ealing Technical College, now part of West London University. The college had pioneered a business studies course which covered bookkeeping, shorthand, and typing, as well as office management in English, French, and Spanish. Finally, I could acquire the skills necessary to survive on my own. The college had a good reputation, and companies were eager to hire its graduates.

Fortuitously, my mother relocated to London the year I started my studies, and I moved in with her.

I enjoyed living in the capital and joined the International Club in West London. The owner asked me if I was interested in some part-time work.

"Of course," I said. "What kind of part-time work?"

"It's only for a few days, but I need someone with perfect French and good manners."

"I'm interested if I can do it."

"I think you can. I'll get back to you with the details."

A couple of days later, he called me to his office to explain what the job entailed.

"The President of the Cameroon, Ahidjo, is paying a state visit to London. He will be received by the Queen at Buckingham Palace, and he'll be staying at the Dorchester Hotel as Her Majesty's guest. You will be his personal assistant."

I was overcome by a mixture of emotions—joy, doubt, uncertainty, and amazement. I had my own office, just outside the Cameroon President's private suite. My job was to keep out unwanted visitors, answer the phone, and keep his diary. In other words, I was the Cerberus guarding the inner sanctum.

A state visit is a very grand affair and culminates in a state banquet. There is a great deal of ceremonial pomp and circumstance. Mid-afternoon, a rather gruff gentleman with a florid complexion barged into my office.

"Hello, how can I help you?" I said.

"I'm here to see His Excellency and Madame Ahidjo."

"Do you have an appointment?"

"I don't need one," he growled.

"I'm sorry, but unless you have an appointment, they are not free to see you." I tried to sound officious and act as if I were about to bar his way. He reminded me of a bulldog ready to charge.

"I'm here on behalf of Her Majesty to inform them of the rules and protocol of meeting the Queen this evening," he blurted.

As if I was supposed to know what he was about. *Why didn't you say so from the start?*

"I see. I'll let them know you're here," I said.

On the day of the state banquet, Madame Ahidjo gave the dress she was going to wear that evening to the hotel laundry. It was a beautiful soft blue chiffon. Later that day, a very nervous little man came up to me and, with trembling hands, showed me a burn mark on her dress. He was very distressed—he had scorched it during ironing. It was my job to let her know. I felt sorry for him, knowing he feared his job was at stake.

However, Mme. Ahidjo was kind and gracious. She reassured him she had another dress and that he was not to worry. I don't think she reported the accident.

I enjoyed my time working at the Dorchester for the Cameroon President. It helped me realize that I could be free and independent of my father's control.

Even before my final college exams, I landed a job in East London with one of the biggest international chemical companies. I was translating and writing up their chemical formulae, and taking dictation and shorthand in several languages. My very first full-time job! At last! I was earning the princely sum of £13 per week.

I was, for my age, fairly naïve and innocent. I would bounce into the offices of the male managers and announce, "I'm here to take down your French letters. Who needs a French letter?"

Finally, a kind older manager took me aside and explained that it was not the right expression for a young lady to use.

I asked him, "Why? I'm the only one who is able to write and translate French. What's wrong with that? I write all the French letters and formulae."

"Yes, I know," he said, "but I think you don't realize that a 'French letter' is slang for a condom."

I shall be forever thankful to him for putting me straight.

Once Dad realized that I had no intention of returning to Cyprus, he was furious. By then, he had married his Austrian girlfriend, Luise, who described the scene to me. She needn't have bothered. I could imagine the rage, the swearing, and the apoplectic reaction. He could not get his head around the fact that he could no longer control me. He went around the house breaking things, kicking and shouting.

I called him, thinking he might be glad that I had a good job. I suppose I was still craving some kind of praise or recognition. I hoped he would be proud of me.

"Dad, guess what! I have a wonderful job with one of the top chemical companies in London. I can now put to good use everything I learned in college."

"Don't talk to me about jobs. Your place is here. Come home."

"But Dad, this is a great opportunity for me..."

"I don't care. Come home or there'll be nothing for you. Not a penny. Nothing."

"But Dad..."

"Not a penny! Do you understand? The only thing you'll get from me is a one-way airfare to Cyprus. That's all you can expect from me."

This was no veiled threat. It was real. I knew he meant it. But my freedom and independence were more important to me than his money.

I had been hoping against hope that he would find it in his heart to be pleased—and even happy for me. That was never to be. I stayed with that company for about a year, and what's more, I proved to myself that I could stand on my own two feet. I had grown wings, and I could fly!

***

I found the ticket to one of the best jobs of my working career in the classified section of *The London Times*. My mother's youngest sister, Aunt Mary, had married Captain Ian Thompson, an officer in the British Army. When they visited me in London, Uncle Ian drew my attention to an ad in *The Times*. The BBC (British Broadcasting Corporation) was looking for a French and Greek monitor for its outpost at Caversham Park.

At the time, I had no idea where Caversham Park was, nor what the BBC did there. I had little confidence in myself, and I almost did not apply—but, in a leap of faith, I responded to the ad. That set in motion a lengthy hiring process that began with a six-hour battery of tests in Greek and French at the BBC's Broadcasting House in central London. After what seemed like an endless wait of several weeks, I was then summoned for an interview at Caversham Park, on the county borders of Berkshire and Oxfordshire.

I received detailed instructions on how to get there from Paddington Station (no, I did not see the Bear there) to Reading (pronounced "Redding") Station. From there, I was to take a taxi or bus to Caversham Park. They would reimburse me for the fare.

On the appointed day, I arrived at Reading Station and got into a cab.

"Where to, luv?" the cabbie asked.

"Caversham Park, please."

"So, you're going to the hush-hush place then?"

"What?"

"Haven't seen you before. Are you a new one?" He was certainly the chatty type.

"I'm going for a job interview."

"You gonna be one of 'em spies then?"

"What are you talking about?"

"Aw! It's all hush-hush. That's where they spy on them Rooskies..."

All this, while driving me to this mysterious spy centre. I thought he was nuts. After about ten or fifteen minutes, we turned into the long driveway of a stately home.

"'Ere we are, luv. Good luck!" And with that, he decanted me in front of a huge door that could have fitted a grand piano going through sideways.

Once inside, I approached the uniformed man behind a desk and told him I was there for an interview. He immediately got up and ushered me through another set of doors and into an elevator. I was met by a secretary on the second floor, who took me to the interview room.

I shall never forget that interview. It was in a big room—or so it seemed to me at the time. At the far end, about five or six people sat in front of a long table, with a single chair placed in front of them, where they invited me to sit. I felt like I was in the dock, facing judge and jury.

My interrogators tried to put me at ease. They asked whether I knew what the BBC Monitoring Service did, and then explained that it was a listening post, gathering news and information from broadcasting stations worldwide. They were hiring linguists to listen to foreign broadcasts, translate, edit, and supply the information to news bureaux, the media, and other customers.

After that, two other interviewers took over and fired questions at me in French and Greek. Fluent in both, I relaxed and answered their questions in either language. At the end of the interview, they said: "Thanks for coming. We'll let you know."

As I left, I couldn't help feeling that the people in this majestic house, with its beautiful grounds, would never hire someone like me. They looked so capable and knowledgeable. Why would they hire a young snippet of a girl when I was sure, they had plenty of other, better-qualified candidates? In the back of my mind, I also worried that the background checks would reveal my illegitimate birth. I still felt that stigma.

Jobs with the BBC were much sought after and carried a lot of prestige. People rarely left the organization, retiring after years of service with a good pension. The BBC was often referred to as "Aunty" because of its patriarchal attitude towards its employees. It was fairly common for several generations of the same family to work there. Nepotism thrived. It was very difficult to get in unless you knew someone already working there or, as in my case, had the expertise they needed.

To my great surprise and delight, several weeks later, I received a letter offering me the job. The starting salary was more than double what I was earning with the chemical company. I got the news the same week President Kennedy was assassinated—November 1963. In December, I started my new job.

The history of Caversham Park goes back to Norman times, and it's even mentioned in the Domesday Book. Over the centuries, the estate was passed down to various members of the British aristocracy.

In April 1786, Thomas Jefferson, accompanied by his close friend John Adams, visited Caversham Park in search of inspiration for his gardens at Monticello. Jefferson made detailed notes of the estate and his impressions. Over the years, royalty visited Caversham Park and were entertained there, including Queen Elizabeth I. During the English Civil War (1642–1651), King Charles I was held prisoner in the grounds. The present building, inspired by Italian Baroque architecture, was erected in 1850. The BBC purchased the property and moved its Monitoring Service there in the spring of 1943.

The orangery was converted into a canteen. Broadcasting is a 24/7 business, and as we covered many overseas stations in different time zones, it was good to be able to have a cup of tea or a hot meal during our working shift.

Finally, I had my dream job. Serendipity had smiled at me. Each day, I looked forward to going to work. My colleagues, the other linguists, dubbed me "the mini-monitor" since I was both small and the youngest. To be at the center of news, views, and current affairs at the height of the Cold War opened up a whole new world for me. It was an interesting and exciting time. I never knew what would turn up on the massive worldwide news circuit. We were the hub of information coming in, which we then disseminated to the outside world.

Of course, I tried to impress my father, but he remained distant and indifferent. I continued to reach out to him, but it was only after I told him that I was "going out" with a male colleague that he called me.

"Who is this young man of yours?" he asked.

"He's not *my* young man, Dad. He's just a colleague, and we go out sometimes."

Alan and I had gone out on a few dates, and we seemed to have similar interests and tastes. My father had not changed and assumed his customary role of inquisitor and accuser.

"Who is he? Where did you meet him?" he asked. "What are his intentions? What's his job? How much does he earn? What are his prospects?"

"Dad, he's just a colleague. We've been out together a few times, and he seems very nice."

"Seems... What do *you* know about men? What do you mean *seems*?"

"He appears to be a decent chap, and I happen to like him."

Dad insisted on meeting "my young man," and before I knew it, had landed at Heathrow Airport. He called from London, gave me the name and address of his hotel, and summoned Alan and me to meet him there.

His sudden interest in my young man was in great contrast to his previous indifference, his threats to cut me off, and his insistence that I return to Cyprus.

Before we went to meet him, I had to prepare Alan and warn him that my father would be grilling him. I tried to explain that it was Dad's way of demonstrating parental concern.

The meeting was not as daunting as I had feared, and Alan and my father seemed to hit it off. At least there were no threats or shouting from Dad. He could turn on the charm when he wanted to, and he could be a good host. He took us out to dinner, all the while asking both direct and indirect questions. To his credit, Alan remained polite and respectful.

In 1965, Alan and I were married in the Greek Orthodox Cathedral in London. I was not expecting any financial help from my father, and he offered none. He realized that with my marriage, I was putting down firm roots in England. My home was now with my husband, career, and children. The last controlling hold he had on me—money—was broken.

Since we both had good, secure jobs, Alan and I started making the rounds of banks and building societies in our efforts to finance the purchase of our first home. During the interviews, after the initial introductions, I became "invisible." All questions were addressed to Alan.

After a while, I'd venture to say: "I too have a job with the BBC. I have a good salary, so we have double income and..."

"Oh no! We don't take the wife's salary into account," came the swift reply from the man—usually always a man—behind the desk.

"Why?"

"Do you plan to have a family?"

"Yes, of course, eventually."

"Well, there, you see. Once you have children, you'll stop earning."

This was emphatically stated by the male managers, who believed that a married woman with kids had to stay at home and be just a housewife. It was years before the Equal Opportunity and Sex Discrimination Acts.

After knocking on several banks and building societies' doors, we finally managed to obtain a mortgage.

By that time, both my mother and father had remarried. Mum had married Jack, an Englishman she met in East Africa, and my father had married Luisa from Vienna. Both Mum and Dad came to my wedding, but their relationship remained frosty. My father stayed in Cyprus, and my mother and Jack retired on the English south coast. After all these years, Mum got her wish and had that much-coveted wedding band on her finger. She retained her spunky, devil-may-care attitude to the end. She often said that the difficult life she had with my father made her bitter and hard—and perhaps there was some truth in that.

Dad divorced Luisa after he got tired of her. Years later, at the age of ninety-three, he married his carer—a woman he imported from Minsk in Belarus. She was fifty years younger, and on his death in 2004, she became his main beneficiary. He never forgave me for not returning to Cyprus, always blaming my mother rather than his behavior. For my part, I never regretted my decision.

Looking back through the prism of time and greater maturity, I see both my parents as damaged individuals, defined by their difficult circumstances and family dysfunction. It was a different era. They made their choices—some good, some bad—and had to live with the consequences.

Once I realized that I also had choices, I chose my own trajectory. There comes a time in life when we realize that we do have control over our destiny. With control comes responsibility. Realizing this gave me the freedom to move on without regrets or recrimination.

Both Alan and I took our marriage vows seriously. His mother died when he was eight, and I lost my mother when I was eleven. We were determined to create the kind of home and family we both had missed.

Perhaps, in some ways, I found validation in marriage, and in the art of balancing career and motherhood. I threw myself wholeheartedly into homemaking. I had no role models, so I relied on magazines, books, and learning from friends.

In the next few years, we had two children, and I continued to work at the BBC. I realized that I was not the stay-at-home type. I had an interesting job that I enjoyed. It enabled us to maintain a good standard of living. I proved the bank managers wrong—not all married women with children abandon their careers.

However, I did feel guilt—torn between work and children. At times, my sense of guilt was exacerbated by comments from other stay-at-home moms.

"We prefer to take care of our children," they said. Or, "Don't you miss out on not being there to see your boys growing up?"

Until another female friend said to me one day: "Take no notice of their snide comments. They would give their right eye to have what you have, but haven't the education or ability to do what you're doing."

It was a strange era: it would have been easier—and even more acceptable—for me to don a flowery skirt and join the anti-Vietnam marches, balancing a baby on my hip, or living in a hippie commune, than to seriously pursue a career.

The BBC was an "equal opportunity" employer (ahead of legislation), but could terminate my contract if they felt that my kids impeded my performance. It had no nursery facilities or lactation rooms. The Equal Opportunity Act was still a few years away.

It was the sixties—the era of hippies, the Beatles, free love, and student rebellions—but women were still expected to fulfill traditional roles. The BBC offered generous maternity leave, but with each pregnancy, I had to sign a document stating that I would return to work under the same conditions as before. They covered their bases. In other words, I could not ask for leave for family reasons.

Since I had such an interesting and fulfilling career, our solution was to hire a live-in nanny. We had several over the years. As I worked shifts, this was by far the best and most practical way to solve the child-minding dilemma.

Despite my friend's wise words, I continued to feel guilty. Having a full-time job—and especially a career—in the mid-1960s was not the norm for women. From time to time, this guilt tempted me to consider giving up work and becoming a full-time housewife. The term *homemaker* did not exist at the time. But on the two occasions when I stayed home on maternity leave, I could not wait to get back to work.

The tedium of changing diapers, cleaning the house, the lack of adult company or conversation during the day, and the relentless, repetitive chores of cooking, cleaning, and gardening were driving me up the wall. Much as I loved my family, I needed something more. I missed the hustle and bustle and excitement of being at the listening post of world events. I needed that drug—I had become a news and current affairs addict.

It was not merely financial need that kept me in the job market, but also my lack of passion for domesticity. I was glad for all the new appliances on the market—the latest models of vacuums, washing machines, dishwashers, and new cleaning products, which I happily bought for my housekeeper.

As long as the children were well cared for by loving nannies, I had peace of mind. After work, I always enjoyed quality time with my family. My work at the BBC did not interfere with motherhood, and I kept the two—career and motherhood—in separate compartments. Not easy, but I proved it could be done.

***

My cooking skills at the time were zero. Soon after we got married, I put a couple of eggs on the gas stove to boil while I went shopping. By the time I returned, the eggs had exploded—smearing the walls and ceiling—and the aluminum pot had partly melted over the range. Egg on the walls and egg on my face. However, I was a quick learner. I copied and collected recipes.

In the sixties, there were still independent butchers in most towns and villages. The Jennings Bros literally saved my bacon in my early forays into cooking. I would describe the dish to Mr. Jennings, our local butcher, and he would tell me the cut of meat I needed. He also advised me how to prepare and cook it.

I asked him why we didn't have the same lean and trimmed cuts of meat I had seen in Germany or France.

"That's the way they prepare their meats over there," he replied. "All the trimmings—fat and gristle—are ground up and used for making their sausages. The Bratwurst, charcuterie, and salamis you see contain all the discards from the lean chops and steaks."

This was years before my cardiologist advised against processed meats.

Eventually, large supermarkets—with their own butcher sections—forced the Jennings Bros out of business. It was the end of an era for a family that had produced generations of butchers and given excellent service.

It was also the end of door-to-door milk deliveries. Milk was now available at the supermarket in cartons or plastic. No more clanking bottles and a cheery "Good morning" from the milkman. Mr. Pilgrim, who used to make weekly deliveries of fruit and vegetables in his van, retired. He, too, could not compete with the increasing number of ethnic fruit and vegetable shops catering to the changing tastes of the nation.

With post-war prosperity, manufacturing companies imported labor from the colonies—Africa, the Caribbean, and Asia. The immigrants brought their recipes and foods, and soon ethnic shops and restaurants sprang up everywhere. Even English pubs added curry, Thai, and Greek dishes to their traditional fare of fish and chips and roast beef. By the turn of the century, the most popular takeout meal in the UK was Indian curry, followed by kebabs and gyro. These days, when Brits go out for a meal, they will say, "Let's go for an Indian," or "Let's go for a Chinese," without considering these dishes exotic. They have become part of the British fare.

In the sixties, freezers began appearing in homes. We bought our first chest freezer through a salesman who came to our home to explain the benefits of ownership. We didn't need much convincing—especially when he told us that the freezer would come full of frozen food.

He also offered a "freezer plan." This guaranteed that our freezer would never be empty and would be continually stocked by his company. We did not take him up on the freezer plan offer. As soon as our own garden yielded produce, I learned to make jams, chutneys, and stocked the freezer with homemade pies.

***

We led an active social life. Our BBC colleagues were party animals, and we enjoyed our get-togethers. After a few drinks, the Russians grew misty-eyed, singing their mournful songs about the Volga boatman who drowned his wife, the Poles danced the polka, and the rest of us joined in—depending on how much we had imbibed.

Alan and I were young, ambitious, and in love. I encouraged him to write books and articles in his spare time, aside from his BBC work. I gave him the space and time to do this. Our only table served as his desk, my sewing space, and our dining table.

Alan began to move up the management ladder. In 1971, he got his big break when he was appointed bureau chief of the BBC Monitoring Service in Hong Kong. This was a great opportunity for him. I agreed to resign to make his career promotion possible. At the time, I felt that his job was more important than mine. Looking back, I wonder if I would make the same decision today—resign from my dream job.

Perhaps, too, the lure of the Far East produced a feeling of adventure. Leaving behind the familiar and routine to embark on something new and relatively unknown was exciting. We took the plunge and went into super-active mode: finding tenants for our home, learning about schools in Hong Kong, shopping for the tropics, and storing personal belongings and furniture. Then came the packing—and then some more packing.

The boys would be starting their first elementary school in the British Crown Colony of Hong Kong. And as soon as we got there, we would be experiencing our first typhoon.

CHAPTER THREE

HONG KONG

After a long and tiring flight in late April 1971, we arrived in Hong Kong. The first thing that hit me was the heat. A blast of hot, humid air enveloped us like a gush of heat from a furnace. Fatigue and hours of sitting in cramped conditions made everything seem surreal. My skin felt clammy, and soon, pools of perspiration were visible on our faces and clothes.

During the taxi ride from Kai Tak Airport to our hotel, we were met by a cacophony of traffic noise, smells, heat, and bright, glaring colors. Even our children, eyes wide open, craned their necks to take it all in.

Laundry draped over bamboo poles greeted us like bunting from every building, balcony, and alcove. Right away, we knew what the local population wore—both outerwear and underwear. But the most lingering impression was the one that assailed my olfactory senses—the smell of cooking. It was overwhelming, and to this day, the smell of fried ginger and garlic does something to my salivary glands. I didn't know it at the time, but we were about to embark on an amazing culinary experience.

Hong Kong was one of the few remaining bastions of the British Empire. After China lost a series of wars, it was forced to release Hong Kong to Britain in 1898, under a 99-year lease agreement. The Chinese always referred to this as an unequal treaty—one of several it had to sign with Western powers.

The BBC had arranged for us to stay at the Repulse Bay Hotel on Hong Kong Island while our apartment was made ready. That first week in a seaside hotel was bliss, as it gave us all time to acclimate, and Alan time to ease into his new job. While we were in the hotel, we experienced our first typhoon.

As it approached and the winds picked up, the staff scuttled about bringing in potted plants, deck chairs, tables—anything that might be blown away. They boarded up windows, and guests were warned to stay indoors, away from the glass. The sky took on a menacing steel-gray color, and there was panic and a sense of urgency in the air.

Across from the hotel, the waves rose with increasing ferocity and the spume stretched across the beach, trying to reach our hotel. Fortunately, this typhoon—named Wanda—was not a direct hit. That was to come a few months later with Typhoon Rose. Wanda brought heavy rain and landslides.

The following day, we woke up to debris, mudslides, seaweed, and sand all over the hotel verandas, flowerbeds, and open spaces. The beach lost its appeal with all the filth and dirt deposited by the storm, including plastic bags, sewage, and dead fish.

Landslides cut off our hotel from the rest of the island. It was also the day we had arranged to meet with the headmistress of the children's primary school. Telephone lines were down, but since the entire island had been affected, we assumed she'd understand our predicament.

After several hours, when part of the road was cleared, a cab driver agreed to take us to the school. It was quite a ride—he had to circumvent boulders, big chunks of mud, and tree trunks that partly blocked the road.

When we arrived at the school, we were greeted by Miss Handyside, the headmistress.

"You are late!" she said.

"Sorry, Miss Handyside, we couldn't get through. The road was blocked."

"Well, you should have called."

This led to more apologies from us, explaining that the lines were down. After we got to meet other parents, we learned that Miss Handyside had a reputation for being strict with parents—she was good at making us feel uncomfortable and ill at ease. But the children liked her. Iain and Alistair became fond of her, so we put up with her brusque manner.

The colony was run along British colonial and administrative lines, roughly modeled on the Westminster system. The judicial system was based on English law, but there was also Chinese customary law, which took second place to English law.

After years of colonial rule and empire-building, the British had learned that in some cases, local law was preferable—and more expedient—when it came to adjudicating family matters relating to concubines and polygamy for Chinese residents.

The BBC apartment, though not large, had servants' quarters in the rear. It was in the Mid-Levels district, and we enjoyed a magnificent view of Hong Kong Harbor. My two main concerns were to settle the boys in their new school, and for me to find something to do. I was not used to having so much spare time.

We had a live-in amah—the name given to servants—and I needed to find something to do.

Ah-Chu, our amah, was a great cook and loved the boys. She had a happy disposition, and nothing was too much work for her. Sunday was her only day off. She did the shopping, cooked, cleaned, did the laundry, and expertly draped it over bamboo poles to dry over her very own balcony in the back.

We woke up every morning to freshly laundered and ironed clothes. On the few occasions when I ventured into the kitchen, she booted me out. I had a hard time convincing her that it was not her kitchen—but mine.

"Missy, you no come—my kitchen."

"Ah-Chu, this is not your kitchen. It's my kitchen."

"No, Missy, you no come in. No Missy in kitchen. Missy sit. Missy go out."

"Ah-Chu, I need a glass of water..."

"I bring. Missy out my kitchen!"

There seemed to be an invisible boundary between the rest of the apartment, the kitchen, and the servants' quarters. I had been warned by other expat wives that good amahs were becoming a dying breed. The new factories—with regular hours and better pay—enticed young girls away from servitude. If you happened to have a good one, she was either poached by someone offering more money, or she left of her own accord for a factory job. For this reason, I didn't want to upset her by insisting on my rights in the kitchen.

One day I asked her, "Ah-Chu, how long have you been working for Western people?"

"Long, long time, Missy."

"How many years?"

"Long, long time. Maybe thirty."

"Have you ever worked for a Chinese family?"

"Ay ya! No, Missy. No work for Chinese."

"Why?"

"No good, Missy."

"Why?"

"No good. English, good boss. Chinese, bad boss."

I also discovered that she kept her culinary secrets and would never divulge a recipe. Whenever I ventured to cook something, however (usually on her day off), she demanded to know how I did it and what ingredients I used.

One day, when I was going to the post office to mail all our Christmas cards, Ah-Chu asked me if I would mail a letter for her. She even gave me the money for the stamp, which I refused.

"No problem, Ah-Chu. I'll put a stamp on it and mail it for you."

"Thank you. Missy very kind."

"It must be important, Ah-Chu. I'll take care of it."

"It's boy meet girl. I matchmake. I good matchmake."

"Oh, I see... You're a matchmaker."

"I good maker. Yes, Missy."

That's how I found out that, in addition to working for us, she acted as a marriage broker. Matchmaking is a time-honored tradition in Chinese culture, and the services of a good matchmaker are highly sought after, especially in arranged marriages. A matchmaker would also be called upon to find a second, third, or even fourth wife for a man. Although the British administration banned concubinage in 1971, the custom still prevailed among the Chinese.

I mailed her letter. A few weeks later I asked, "Ah-Chu, have you heard back about the matchmaking? Is there going to be a wedding?"

"Ay ya! No, Missy. No good."

"Why?"

"No good, Missy. Bad Feng Shui!"

"What happened? Bad Feng Shui? How?"

I knew the Chinese—especially Ah-Chu's generation—were superstitious. All the signs had to be propitious for most activities and decisions. Even the British administration, before laying down the foundations of a new building, would invite a Chinese Feng Shui practitioner to detect the most auspicious placement of the structure— where to put the front door and which way the building should face. The Chinese staff hesitated and even refused to enter a building with "bad" Feng Shui.

My curiosity was roused. I wanted to know how it was bad Feng Shui for this particular couple.

"How is it bad Feng Shui, Ah-Chu?"

"Stamp. Wrong. Missy."

"You mean I put the wrong stamp on your letter? I put the right amount. I asked the post office and they gave me the stamp."

"No, Missy. Stamp wrong way."

Finally, it dawned on me. As the letter was addressed in Chinese and I couldn't read the characters, I had placed the stamp in the wrong position—upside down. This created bad luck. I had ruined a young couple's chance of happiness. I felt terrible.

Ah-Chu, however, was not concerned. She simply shrugged her shoulders and said, "Bad Feng Shui, bad marriage," she said.

"Better luck next time. No worry, Missy. Maybe best this way."

Our sons, Iain and Alistair, loved their school in Hong Kong, and they thrived there. Glenealy Junior School had a good reputation. Iain, who had received speech therapy back in England, came first in an island-wide poetry recitation—this was in his first year of elementary school. Alistair soon followed his older brother there, and both enjoyed school. They also loved the beach and picnics on the island. Even today,

I can see them building sandcastles and running into the surf in the South China Sea.

I made my first friend outside the school gates. Sue and I started chatting as we waited for our kids to come out of school. Her husband, Peter, worked for the government. She was tall and slim with beautiful eyes. She told me she was a Christian Scientist and that every day she read from Mary Baker Eddy's literature. She had two children about the same age as mine, and she had been in Hong Kong longer. I was glad to learn about life in the colony from her.

Both Sue and I took sewing lessons from Mrs. Chan, who taught us how to make patterns and create our own designs. She had a huge table in her apartment and was very particular that nothing was wasted. She saved every scrap of material and even discarded pins that we had carelessly dropped on the floor.

The colony was famous for its many tailors. With fine silk, cashmere, and wool at very low prices, business was brisk. Many hotels had resident tailors who offered to make a suit or cocktail dress "very cheap" and deliver it within a few hours. We repeatedly warned our guests about these "specials," as the workmanship and finish were not as good as with a suit made over several days.

One of our visitors from Washington, D.C., ignored our advice. He had a three-hour suit made. Back in D.C., while attending a formal function, a fellow guest remarked that a piece of thread was sticking out of his shoulder seam. When she tried to remove it, the entire sleeve came off—leaving him sleeveless in the presence of other dignitaries. He even had the chutzpah to write to us and complain!

It was so tempting to write back and say, "We told you so."

***

Sue had no luck with her amah (amahs and their escapades were a frequent subject of conversation among expat wives). She had a "makeye-learn amah."

"What's a 'makeye-learn' amah, Sue?"

"These are young girls from the villages or new arrivals from mainland China. They don't know any English, or very little, and have no education. Most of them are illiterate."

"So how can they work for you?"

"They're a lot less expensive than the older, experienced amahs. They're grateful for free board and lodging, and you train them."

"Do you train them to cook and clean?"

"Something like that. Usually they know how to cook—Chinese food mostly. I teach them how to use the washing machine, the dishwasher, and the vacuum. I also give them time to go to school to learn English."

"That's a great idea."

"Well... it works sometimes, but there can be problems. I've sometimes found that she put the laundry in the dishwasher and the dishes in the washing machine. As for the vacuum, she used the wrong end and spread dust and dirt all over the place instead of sucking it up. And as soon as they pick up enough English, they leave to work in a factory."

"I see. I'd better hang on to Ah-Chu, then."

"Yes. She has a reputation for being a good cook. You know about double pay, don't you?"

"No. What's that?"

"It's the custom here to give them two months' pay for Chinese New Year. It's the only time they take a holiday, and most of them visit family in China."

"You mean two months' pay?"

"Yep. Often, they take the money and disappear. They move on to another household with more pay."

"I see..."

I didn't really see, but we managed to keep Ah-Chu during our tour of duty in Hong Kong. I guess she considered us good employers. Also, she was devoted to the children.

During Chinese New Year, a mass exodus of Hong Kong Chinese visited relatives in mainland China. Ah-Chu was one of them. For weeks before her departure, her quarters were heaving with stuff—bags of rice, dehydrated fruit, jars filled with food and vegetables, even bicycle tires and other bits and pieces. I never thought that a small, elderly woman could carry all that on her own. I asked her why the tires and other bicycle parts. She explained that her relative needed them because he couldn't find replacements in the People's Republic.

On the appointed day, she balanced a long bamboo pole across her shoulders, and all the accumulated "stuff" dangled from it, secured in plastic bags. It must have weighed a ton. That's how she would cross the border—laden like a beast of burden. She delivered the goods and, after a couple of days, returned with tea and other local food delicacies from her village. She repeated this ritual every year. I had a sneaking suspicion that some of that stuff was used to bribe the border guards.

Like me, Sue was not content to be merely a homemaker. She wanted to build her own beauty business and was in the throes of experimenting with creams, treatments, and massage. I was a willing guinea pig and enjoyed numerous facials and tests of her products.

We lost touch after we left the Far East, until 2018, when we reconnected through social media. I was not surprised to hear that she had become a successful entrepreneur and developed a skincare line she called *Susan Molyneux*, which was marketed by more than 1,500 beauty salons in the UK. She is also a successful author, and I read with great interest her books *Tea at Sam's*, *Making Scents*, and *Stories to Go*.

In the '70s, Hong Kong had prospered under British administration. It was an important international trading center. Some predicted that this prosperity couldn't last and that China would take it over. Others said, "Why would China kill the goose that lays golden eggs?" Hong Kong was not due to revert to China until 1997. In the '70s, that seemed a long way off—and in the meantime, there was a lot of money to be made.

China was still suffering from the aftereffects of the Cultural Revolution, and it would be at least another couple of decades before the Dragon would stir and rise again. We heard stories about people who fled the mainland, risking their lives in shark-infested waters or facing the firing squads of the Red Guards in an effort to reach Hong Kong. To them, Hong Kong meant freedom and a job.

On the other side of the "Bamboo Curtain," the Chinese Communist government tried its best to prevent them from leaving. Those caught were severely punished—often with death.

Even after the establishment of diplomatic relations with the US, foreign journalists were not welcome in China, and the doors remained closed. The Foreign Office discouraged us from visiting because they could not guarantee our safety. Hence, the importance of Hong Kong as a listening post. Everyone on our side of the Bamboo Curtain had their eyes peeled on the mainland and their ears firmly pressed against that invisible wall, trying to snatch tidbits of information about what was happening on the other side.

The Foreign Correspondents' Club was a second home to all journalists based in the colony. It became our second home as well. It was rampant with rumors, news, views, speculation, and conjecture.

The Vietnam War was also coming to an end. Most journalists covered Southeast Asia as well as the Far East. Our journalist friends spent weeks, even months, in Saigon covering the war, while their wives stayed behind. It was akin to being a military wife with a husband deployed to a war zone. It put great stress on marriages, and some did not survive.

When Saigon fell to the Viet Cong in April 1975, the only foreign correspondent who stayed behind was the BBC's Brian Barron. He and his wife Angie were our friends, and I remember how worried and concerned we were for his safety. He watched as the last helicopter left the rooftop of the US embassy compound in Saigon. Disobeying BBC orders to evacuate, Brian stayed behind. In fact, it was quite a coup, as he continued to file story after story despite the Communist takeover. For some unknown reason, he was allowed to send out news. His dispatches from that period are now in the historic archives of the BBC. When he eventually returned to Hong Kong, he regaled us with the stories he couldn't send under the Viet Cong. He described the messy and chaotic evacuation of Americans and their allies—later so well depicted by Ken Burns in his 2017 documentary *The Vietnam War*. We already had the scoop from Brian. He went on to win numerous awards for his reporting.

Aside from foreign correspondents, Hong Kong attracted many interesting characters—entrepreneurs, traders, adventurers, writers, seekers of something different—looking for a more exciting lifestyle. Like many other colonies, it also attracted the arrivistes, the parvenus, and snobs. Life in the colony afforded them a better and higher standard of living. At the very top of the social ladder were the "old China hands."

They were often first- or second-generation expats, born in Hong Kong, Shanghai, Qingdao, or another Treaty Port, and who, after WWII, had moved to Hong Kong to get away from the turmoil in mainland China.

The expat lifestyle can be seductive and contagious with its endless cocktail parties and social gatherings. It was also cliquish. I soon discovered that people tended to socialize and party with colleagues from their departments. Those in the Public Works Department tended to party together, the military with the military, diplomats with diplomats, and journalists with journalists. Journalists and China watchers fed off each other, exchanged stories—or kept them to themselves—so they could score the first scoop.

One notch above the correspondents were the China watchers who had made China their special field of interest. Foreign correspondents always sought them out and looked to them for advice and information. One of them was a Jesuit priest, Father Laszlo Ladany. Before he settled in Hong Kong, he had lived in China for many years. He was the Vatican's eyes and ears for the region. He was fluent in Mandarin and Cantonese and was also a strong critic of the Communist government. Many journalists tapped into his knowledge, which he gladly shared. I was told he also kept a good cellar. He had an encyclopedic knowledge of China, its people, and traditions. He was up to date with developments behind the Bamboo Curtain, and his predictions were usually spot on.

Like Sue, I was not content to get onto the endless cocktail merry-go-round or spend hours lying beside the pool at the Ladies' Recreation Club. Neither did I wish to confine myself to the interests and activities of the expat white ghetto. I needed something more. I wanted to immerse myself in the local culture and make friends from a wider circle. Since our sons were settled in school and our amah, Ah-Chu, proved to be good at her job, with Alan's support, I enrolled at Hong Kong University, which was a branch of Oxford University.

Apparently, I was not the only wife with the same idea. Olivia, the wife of the *Time-Life* magazine correspondent, and Rita, the wife of the Reuters bureau chief, were my fellow students. Of the three of us, I was the only one who graduated, since both Rita and Olivia had to leave when their husbands were transferred. The Reuters news agency had purchased a single-story house on the Peak—Hong Kong Island was divided into the Peak, Mid-Levels, and sea level. We envied those lucky enough to live in a house, as opposed to an apartment. The only drawback was that, often, in the early mornings, a cloud enveloped the Peak or hung between our Mid-Levels and the Peak. Most mornings, Rita called me to ask what the weather was like "down below." As well as being a freshman at Hong Kong University, Rita also did the voiceovers for the locally produced kung fu movies starring the legendary Bruce Lee and his stuntman, Jackie Chan.

Galya, one of our BBC colleagues in Caversham, had a married brother in Hong Kong, Gene Yourieff. Gene's family was part of the exodus of White Russians who fled the Reds and settled in Shanghai before the Second World War. When the Japanese attacked China, they came to Hong Kong. Gene and his wife, Tina, made us welcome, and I remember several pleasant evenings spent in their home, including wonderful New Year's Eve parties. They owned a junk boat, and we spent many weekends with them sailing up and down the South China Sea, visiting the surrounding islands.

During the Japanese occupation, Gene was incarcerated, along with other Westerners, in a Japanese prison camp. He came close to death through ill-treatment and starvation. From time to time, when asked, he described some of those harrowing stories of the prison camp. I always admired him for not leaving the Far East after Japan's defeat. I guess his roots were too deeply embedded in China, and Hong Kong was the closest he could be to the mainland.

During my first year in Hong Kong, I decided to invest in contact lenses. I'm nearsighted, and to this day I can thread a needle sans glasses, but I rely on them for distance. At night, I removed them and placed them in a small glass of liquid solution next to my bed. It wasn't long before I woke up one night and gulped them down, thinking I was having a drink of water. I had to buy a second pair. (Over the years I lost and replaced several pairs.)

One evening, when we were having dinner at the American Attaché's home, I realized I was missing one contact lens. Our hostess, Linda, herself a veteran contact lens user, noticed that I was struggling.

"Honey, have you lost a contact lens?"

"Umm. Yes... How did you guess?"

"From the way you place one hand over one eye, and then the other. I do the same when I'm missing one of those blasted things."

We were sitting at their big round dining table, and all the guests (I think there were eight of us) crawled under the table—there were a couple of ambassadors and their wives, plus our hosts—on all fours, searching for my contact lens. Even to this day I get the giggles when I think of it, but at the time, I was mortified.

Despite our efforts under the table, we had no success. Then Linda asked the amahs in the kitchen to drain the soup and search through all the leftover food. Again, no success—and more embarrassment for me. Finally, our hostess said:

"Honey, it could have slipped."

"Slipped? Where?"

"You know, they creep up or down under your eyelid."

I was new to contact lenses, so I didn't know this could happen. Linda took me to the bathroom and found the wretched lens under my eyelid. Lens recovered, but my dignity was not.

Linda and her husband had been in the Far East for several tours of duty. She told us the following story concerning a colleague. The State Department, like the BBC, pays for the transfer and shipping of personal goods at the end of a tour. When this particular colleague returned to the USA, the State Department queried the cost of shipping, which was much higher than usual. He explained that, when he asked if they would ship his junk back home, the State Department agreed. There's likely a Chinese junk boat moored somewhere in a U.S. port or private dock, drawing admiring looks from all who see it. I don't think the State Department will make that mistake again.

At that time, the only way to get from Victoria Island to the Kowloon side was by ferry. The harbor tunnel was planned, but construction had not yet begun. Ferries crisscrossed the harbor at regular intervals both day and night. It was a fun way to travel, but we had been warned that pickpockets were active and were careful to guard our purses and wallets.

Over dinner, on another occasion, a friend described a recent experience he had on the ferry. On his way to his doctor on the Kowloon side, he had in his pocket a "sample" requested by his GP. As luck would have it, he got pickpocketed during the crossing. He arrived at the doctor's surgery empty-handed. The pickpocket had more than what he had bargained for on his hands.

Along with Olivia and Rita, I was making friends with some of my other Chinese fellow students. I often joined them for picnics and outings. During one outing, one of my classmates, Lee Mei Tin, remarked:

"You see that couple walking ahead?"

"Yes. What of them?" I said.

"They're boat people."

"How do you know?"

"From the way they walk. Look."

She explained that the Boat People are born and raised on the many boats—some junks, but mostly sampans—that sail up and down the South China Sea. They live on their boats with their extended family members, as well as their pigs, hens, and other animals. Over the years, they develop a certain gait as they adapt to the constant movement of the boat. Eventually, I too learned to recognize them by the way they walked.

The British administration, believing it was better to house them on land, provided apartments with running hot and cold water, showers, and other modern conveniences. They ordered them off their boats and relocated them to newly built high-rise buildings in the New Territories and on some of the islands.

The experiment failed. The Boat People did not take to their new accommodations. They found the apartments too small to house their pigs, hens, and goats. They were unaccustomed to elevators and suffered from claustrophobia. They also missed the gentle roll and movement underfoot. Even during the dangerous typhoon season, they felt safer in their boats than in the high-rise buildings. Many jumped from the upper floors to their death. The high suicide rate finally convinced the government that forcing them to abandon their traditional lifestyle had been a mistake.

***

"I don't like rice. I hate rice," my three-year-old son, Alistair, declared during the flight to Hong Kong. I thought, *Oh boy. You're in for a surprise.* By the time we left the Far East a few years later, we all enjoyed rice in all its many forms.

China loves to eat. It's a country of foodies. Chinese cuisine consists of a number of regional styles, each unique in flavor and technique. My favorite was the food of the Guangdong region—Cantonese. For the Chinese, food represents more than sustenance. It is deeply ingrained in their culture. There are traditional foods for every special occasion—whether it's Chinese New Year, the birth of a baby, birthdays, the Moon Festival (Moon Cakes), the Dragon Boat Festival, weddings, or even funerals.

Just a few days after our arrival, we quickly realized how important food was when BBC staff invited us out for a meal. It was the beginning of a wonderful culinary adventure. Our hosts explained each dish, its health benefits, the season it belonged to, and the order in which it should be served. Like everything else in China, food follows the Yin and Yang theory. There must be balance. Traditional Chinese medicine emphasizes the effect of food on the body's equilibrium—between cool and warm, dry and damp. Chinese doctors focus more on the medicinal qualities of food than its taste.

One day I had a severe backache, and Ah Chu noticed I was moving with difficulty.

"Missy, I make you better."

"Thanks, Ah Chu. But I think I need to rest. Maybe go see the doctor."

"Missy, I cook for you."

"Ah Chu, you always cook for us."

"No, Missy. This special soup. I make."

After this brief exchange in Chinglish, she went to the market and returned with several small packets. She spent some time in the kitchen—by then I knew better than to stand over her and observe—then she bid me try her soup. I could see mushrooms and bits of chicken floating in the broth. It was tasty.

"Ahh... it's delicious," I said, sensing warmth spread through my body.

"Missy, you like?"

"Yes, Ah Chu. It's wonderful. What's in it?"

Without answering, she offered me a second bowl, which I gladly accepted. After half an hour or so, I noticed my back felt better, and soon the ache was gone.

"Ah Chu, that was wonderful. What was the soup?"

"Snake, Missy."

"Ay yah, Ah Chu! You gave me snake?"

"Yes. Missy like. Missy better."

I had to agree with her.

To this day, snake soup is the most exotic dish I have ever eaten—and I can vouch that it cures backache. At least, it cured mine.

***

It was during this time that the National Organization for Women (NOW) made its appearance in Hong Kong. This was the second wave of feminism, which began in America in the 60s under Betty Friedan. Unlike the first wave, this second wave sought more than universal suffrage. The goal was to enable and empower women with equal rights in the bedroom, the workforce, and the pocketbook.

Years ago, I had read Simone de Beauvoir's book *Le Deuxième Sexe* (The Second Sex), but not Friedan's bestseller *The Feminine Mystique*, which she wrote in 1963. Friedan's book is widely credited with starting the second wave of feminism. She believed that confining women to the home limited them and wasted their talent and potential. According to Friedan, the nuclear family, heavily marketed at the time, did not reflect happiness but instead degraded women.

I attended a couple of NOW meetings on the island. I agreed with the principle that confining women to a homemaker role, depriving them of an education, and limiting them to housekeeping, feeding, and breeding roles was akin to slavery. But something about their strident and angry preaching from the Gospel of Feminism grated with me. These adherents of women's lib were on a mission—to liberate their "sisters" and empower them. I shared my thoughts with some of my Chinese friends.

The more I learned about the culture and traditions of China, the more I realized that NOW and its objectives did not meet the needs of the people it targeted. The advocates of American feminism had failed to do their homework and study the history and importance of the family in Asia. While the nuclear family remains a Western and relatively new concept, in China the family was never nuclear. It was much more than just mum, dad, and kids. It consisted of grandparents, aunts and uncles, nephews and nieces, second and third wives, and their children. As in most families, there is a pecking order, but as one dynamic unit, it acts as a bulwark against any outside attack—whether physical, economic, verbal, or otherwise. NOW failed to make inroads into or break up this traditional family system.

The main targets of NOW were polygamy and concubinage. The British had outlawed both in 1971, but they still prevailed. Wealthy men often took a second or third wife or acquired concubines. The reasons varied: some were economic, some for male progeny, and some to assist the first wife in her domestic duties. The custom also provided a kind of protection and made provision for young, single women whose families could not afford to keep them.

As late as November 28, 1999, the Hong Kong-based newspaper *South China Morning Post* published an article entitled "Law Aside, Concubines Still A Necessary Accessory." The British were wise not to insist on its abandonment, as the tradition remained ingrained in Chinese culture. They allowed it to peter out gradually over the years. That was something NOW and its advocates did not understand. Their efforts to bring Western family concepts and American-style feminism to the Far East were bound to fail.

NOW did have some success with expat women. I know of two marriages that broke up because the wife espoused the views and attitudes of angry feminism. Perhaps their marriages were not strong to begin with, and NOW was the catalyst.

***

Call it coincidence or whatever you will, but soon after we arrived in Hong Kong, I was often asked if I knew Jackie Pullinger.

"No. Who is she?"

"She's from England, like you."

Strange how people seem to think that if you're from England or London, you should know everyone living there. "What does she do?" I asked.

"She's a Christian missionary."

I had never heard of her, but I imagined a middle-aged matron with thick ankles, her hair in a tight bun, wearing sensible shoes and dowdy clothes. "No, sorry. I don't know her." Then one day my friend Sue said, "Would you like to hear Jackie Pullinger? She's holding a meeting at the Island School."

"But you're a Christian Scientist, why would you want to hear a Christian missionary?"

"Well, actually I'm not anymore... It'll be worthwhile listening to her. She's doing some interesting work in the Walled City," Sue said.

I had heard of the Walled City on the Kowloon side. It was something of a no-man's land. Even the police didn't venture there unless they went in big numbers and were armed. The triads (Chinese secret societies and gangs) had overall control. The British authorities didn't interfere unless it was essential. I reasoned that if this dowdy old lady went all by herself, she must be something special.

"Okay. Let's go. When's the next meeting?"

"Next Tuesday evening."

We went the following Tuesday. The meeting was held in the school principal's home. The room was big and filled with bodies. People sat on the floor, on chairs, and anywhere there was space. It was summer and the monsoon season had started. The humidity, both inside and outside, was palpable. I also felt a sense of excitement and expectation. A couple of young Chinese guys started strumming their guitars, and the singing began. The tunes were catchy, and the words easy to follow. Most songs were in English, but from time to time, songs were in Chinese. I wondered when the missionary lady would make her appearance. When the singing stopped, a young blonde stood up, and Sue whispered, "That's Jackie!"

"What! This drop-dead gorgeous blonde is the famous Jackie Pullinger?"

"Yep."

Jackie introduced us to her "boys" by name and then asked them to tell their stories. They spoke Cantonese, and an interpreter translated into English. Every one of them had been a drug addict. Most of them belonged to a triad. Triads were like a family to these vulnerable youngsters. The Big Brothers took care of the Little Brothers and initiated them into a life of drugs, prostitution, and crime. There was a joke going around at the time that the Sicilian Mafia had tried to get a foothold in the colony but left after a year, chased out by the Chinese triads. This was the Chinese underworld with its secret societies. Most Europeans on the island lived in their white ghettos and never came into contact with them. The two worlds coexisted side by side, and only a few brave souls crossed over. Jackie Pullinger was one of them.

Suddenly, a young lad was talking excitedly and repeating: "Look at my arms! Look at my arms!" I asked why. I was told that he wanted to show us that he no longer had needle marks. He had been a heroin addict from a very young age, as well as a dealer to support his habit. The interpreter translated for him and said, "Jesus has saved him."

"Look at my arms. Look at my arms," the interpreter was translating.

Why should I look at his arms? I thought. As if she read my thoughts, Sue explained that he had no needle marks on his arms because he had now given up his heroin habit. He was thanking and praising God for setting him free of his addiction. He was glowing, and his passion for his newly acquired faith was self-evident. This was my first encounter with former drug addicts.

I thought: "I am a white, middle-class Christian woman, but this boy loves God more than I do and knows Jesus in a new and personal way that I've never known. I want some of that." This former drug addict had given me a desire for a closer walk with God and a thirst and hunger to know Him better. Up to that time, I thought I was a Christian because I was christened as a baby and sometimes went to church. But these young lads and Jackie had something I lacked, and I definitely wanted it for myself. They had a special and intimate relationship with God. Most of them were illiterate, but they knew Jesus personally and trusted Him in everything. If Jesus could get them off drugs, He could certainly provide all their needs.

That evening was my new birth and my spiritual awakening. It took a former drug addict to open my eyes and heart.

Years later, my father ridiculed my faith and called it a crutch. I thought: Indeed, and what a wonderful crutch—one I can always rely on, a crutch that will not let me down or disappoint. What better! It was this particular crutch that enabled me to navigate life's low points and difficulties. For me, it was more than a crutch; it was the rudder.

After I graduated with a double major in political science and history, I spent the remaining time of our tour learning the mysteries of the Chinese dancing brush, aka Chinese Brush painting (better known in the US as Sumi-e). I fell in love with this ancient art form—a love affair that has lasted to this day. Before leaving the colony in 1977, I stocked up on Chinese brushes, ink, rice paper, and some books. The BBC would ship our stuff (no junk for us) in a couple of containers that would arrive a few weeks after we arrived in the UK.

When the time came to say goodbye to all our Hong Kong friends, we realized how attached we had become to the place—the lifestyle, the travels through the Far East, the stimuli from the cross-pollination of cultures and, yes, I have to admit, finding freshly laundered and ironed clothes by our bedside every morning. How I wish I could take Ah-Chu back to England with me!

CHAPTER FOUR

RETURN TO BLIGHTY

Before returning to Blighty, we decided to visit several countries on our return journey–Thailand, India, Iran, Lebanon, and Cyprus. This was an excellent opportunity to visit other countries and introduce our sons to different cultures.

In Thailand, we visited the tribal people in the Golden Triangle. We saw elephants in the jungle carrying huge trees and logs in their trunks and dropping them in the river to be swept downstream to the mills and factories. The baby elephants loved playing and rolling in the mud while their trainers hosed them down. We had rides on the huge mammals that seemed docile and keen to oblige. Unlike African elephants, the Asian variety can be trained.

The highlight of this trip for our boys was our visit to a snake farm, where they staged fights between a mongoose and a cobra. We watched in great fascination as the cobra was dropped inside the mongoose's glass case. There followed a dance to death. Every time the snake lunged forward, the mongoose deftly moved away. It was attack and defense. The rhythm reminded me of Dance Macabre by Saint Saens. Each time, the mongoose avoided the venomous bites. Finally, the little furry mammal grabbed the snake just behind its head. I guess it was the neck if snakes have necks, that shook it violently. The Thai workers tried to separate them—to keep the cobra alive to fight another day. This time, the mongoose had had enough. It would not let go until the snake was truly dead. As they carried the snake away, I asked what they were going to do with it.

"We take to market. We sell for a good price. It makes good curry."

I made a mental note not to eat curry while in Thailand.

Our next stop was Iran. At the airport, once we cleared customs, we were accosted by someone who seemed keen to attach himself to us. He sidled up to us, "Welcome to Iran," he said. "Thank you for visiting our country. I am from the Interior Ministry, and I am at your service. Where do you want to go?"

"Umm. We're only here for a couple of days. We just want to tour around Teheran. We have already booked our hotel, thank you."

" Well, I am here to take care of you. Anything you need. I am at your service. Will you be going outside Tehran and visiting other cities?"

He wanted to know our itinerary and plans. *He's very curious.* Our passports stated that we were journalists and, most probably, he was a SAVAK (the Shah's secret police) agent assigned to keep an eye on us. At the time, the BBC was in the Shah's bad books since a few months earlier, the BBC correspondent had been asked to leave the country. We did not travel outside Tehran, but we always looked nervously over our shoulders. Were we being followed? During our brief stay, we bought a couple of Persian rugs before flying out to our next destination.

We had pre-booked our hotel in Beirut. A taxi took us from the airport there. The hotel had an impressive entrance and an even more impressive front desk. Somehow, it seemed empty. Perhaps it's not the tourist season. As soon as we paid for our two-day stay, the manager said, "I wouldn't stay here if I were you. We have a civil war going on."

"But you just took the money for our stay. We booked in advance. Why didn't you tell us beforehand while we were making the booking?"

"It's not safe. You have children. Go. You must go. We have a civil war. People are being killed."

It didn't take long to convince us. We could hear gunshots outside. He ordered a taxi, warning us that the road to the airport was dangerous and that the driver would have to find a safe route. He was not exaggerating.

There was pandemonium at Beirut's international airport. It seemed as if the entire population of Lebanon was trying to escape. Our tickets were for later that week, and my heart sank when I saw how many people were vying for plane seats. I noticed several groups of Cypriot tourists returning to Cyprus. I went up to their guide and begged him, in Greek, to get us on board with them. Somehow, he managed to include us in his group. The flight from Beirut to Cyprus took about thirty minutes, and there was only a standing room. I have never flown before, or since, with people standing in the aisles. At least we were leaving the war zone and on our way to stay with my father for a few days before returning to England. I could proudly show him my college degree certificate. Would he be impressed?

Naively, we thought that our return would be straightforward and we'd simply slip back into our old lifestyle. The transition was not smooth. We had changed. Living abroad has that effect on you. The country also had changed. Our sons found it easier to settle in their new schools, although we were not happy with the changes that had taken place in the country's education system.

Life back in the UK was also hard for Alan. In Hong Kong, he was the bureau chief and the boss. Back in the UK, he was another nine-to-five employee.

One of the first things I did on our return was to teach our children to be alert and not to trust strangers. I hated doing this as I felt I was taking away their innocence. I think every parent feels the same way—as our kids grow up, we have to warn and teach them to be careful and not trust other human beings. "Promise me that you'll never, ever get into anyone's car after school," I said.

"Why?"

"Because there are many bad people about it, and they do bad things to children."

"What things?"

"They want to hurt you and take you away. They sometimes kill you. So, if anyone pretends that they are meant to pick you up from school or offer to give you a ride, you do not get into their car. Even if they know us or have been to our home. You do not get into anyone's car!"

I kept repeating this warning and stressing it. It was not paranoia; I was trying to keep my kids safe. It is every parent's nightmare to wait and wait for their offspring to come home and then to have to report a missing child to the police. A few weeks later, my friend and neighbor, Glenys, whose son was in the same class as Alistair, offered to give him a ride home as it was raining. Remembering my dire warnings, he refused and came home soaking wet!

During our years overseas, the Labour Party took control of the government and made some drastic changes to Britain's education system. Under the misguided belief that the previous system was unfair and elitist, they introduced the comprehensive system of education. Students were no longer streamed according to ability. Instead, they were grouped under the misconception that the more able students would help the less able ones. In fact, the opposite occurred: the able kids became bored and tired of waiting for the others to catch up. They lost interest, dropped out, or acted up. The lowest common denominator pulled down the more academic students. It created havoc ill-discipline, and caused teachers to despair.

One day, I was called to the principal's office at my son's elementary school.

"You asked to see me, Headmaster?"

"Yes, please take a seat."

I wondered what terrible misdemeanor my kids had committed.

"During recess the other day, your son went up to a boy in his class and asked him if he was 'Little Black Sambo.'"

He stopped and waited for me to say something. I had no idea what the significance was. So he continued: "This is not a word we use for a black person. It's an insult."

"But my kids love the story of *Little Black Sambo*. It's been a long-time favorite."

"Maybe. But we don't use that word anymore. It's inappropriate."

I tried to explain to him that we'd been living overseas for several years, and my kids did not know about this new political correctness or about the banned vocabulary that had crept in.

"My boys have lived in a multi-cultural environment, Headmaster. In my family, we're all colorblind. The only time I practice apartheid is when I do the laundry and separate the whites from the coloreds."

However, afterward, I explained to the boys that the word "sambo" had different meanings and they should not use it.

It was not the only disagreement I had with this principal. During a weekend-long school trip to the West of England, I found out from another mother that my younger son had been "lost" on Broadmoor in Devon. Neither the school nor my son told me about the incident. I was, to say the least, perturbed and angry that no one had informed me. This time, it was my turn to ask to see the principal. "Why was I not informed of Alistair being lost on Broadmoor?"

"I felt it was not necessary as he was found."

"You mean the teacher turned back and went looking for him?"

"He was found on the moor by a couple of other hikers."

"You mean to tell me that he was found wandering all alone, and two strangers picked him up? How can you lose an 8-year-old from a small group and not notice it?"

"Well, nothing happened. He was brought back to the youth hostel."

At this point, I exploded. I threatened to write to the newspapers and to report the incident to the education authorities. He asked me not to upset the status quo and told me that the teacher involved could lose his job.

"I could have lost my child!" I retorted.

It was this and other similar incidents that caused me to take a postgraduate teaching qualification. I felt I had a duty to change the status quo and raise standards. I planned to become an activist for change to our broken education system. Big head, big ideas.

***

My first teaching job was at the local Comprehensive Secondary School. I was hired as a language teacher, but from time to time, when a colleague was off sick, one of us was asked to take their class. One of our colleagues, Miss Evans, often called in sick. On one of these occasions, I was asked to substitute for her. This was a class of 15-year-olds who were just marking time. The minute they became sixteen, they could leave school. They were not interested in learning, and mentally, they had already left school. They were also a handful. They could not wait to join the hundreds of other high school dropouts. Ten minutes into the lesson (Miss Evans had sent in her lesson plans), a fight broke out at the back of the room. I went next door to get a male teacher who refused to come. Somehow, I managed to calm them down. I had to file a report of the incident. No sooner done, I was called into the assistant principal's office. She didn't beat around the bush: "I hear you had a problem with Miss Evans 'class."

"Well, as you can see from my report, there was a fight among a few of the boys at the back of the class."

"What caused it?"

"I don't know. I gave them Miss Evans 'instructions, and as I was writing up the details on the board, the fight broke out. I tried to get help from the male teacher next door, but he wouldn't come."

"Teachers are not allowed to leave their class unattended. You shouldn't have left the class. You have poor discipline. You have a discipline problem."

This is where I saw red. "Excuse me! I have raised two sons, a husband, and a male dog without any discipline problems. I am not a youngster out of graduate school. This is certainly not *my* discipline problem. I have taught drug addicts and their children at rooftop schools in Hong Kong, and there was never a discipline problem. Those kids, all ages and from the gutter, respected the authority of the teacher and were keen to learn."

She tried to silence me, but I was on a roller coaster of righteous indignation.

"I trained to be a teacher, not an animal trainer or to crack the whip! I did not create a discipline problem. It exists in this school already. I simply inherited it, and you perpetuate it by not supporting your staff and by not imposing good boundaries and rules for the kids. You seem to think that only teachers need to have them."

After that, I had no more problems with her, but I also understood the reason for Miss Evans 'frequent absences. Later, I also learned that she had suffered a nervous breakdown. Those kids were quite capable of giving anyone a nervous breakdown. After my probationary year in the government school sector, I went to teach at a private college, where the classes were small and the students were well-behaved.

I realize now that it was the beginning of a big shift and downgrading of teaching. It was, actually dumbing down. Teachers were now expected to act as social workers, surrogate parents, therapists, and mentors. Teachers were told to befriend their students. Anything but teach. To this effort, the powers that be imposed increasingly heavier administrative duties at the expense of teaching. The needs of young people were being met by a host of others: teachers, counselors, therapists, psychiatrists, and social workers, as the traditional family unit was breaking up. As mum and dad were unavailable or incapable of parenting, others were forced to step in and take up the cudgel.

One of the advantages of teaching was that I had the same holidays and breaks as the boys. It was the one job that fitted in with the demands of a growing—growing in age, not numbers— family.

**

In 1986, Alan was invited to join a group of British Parliamentarians (the UK equivalent to Congressmen) to visit Mongolia. I decided to tag along. I jumped at the opportunity to visit the birthplace of Genghis Khan.

Mongolia was the first Soviet satellite and was dependent on Moscow, both economically and politically. As the Soviet Union started to fall apart, Mongolia began to search for alternative trading partners. The British delegation was there to look into trade possibilities between the two countries. Keen to show off its cultural history, the Mongolian government took great pains to make us welcome. To this end, we visited cashmere and fur factories, the steppes, and the Gobi Desert.

The capital, Ulan Bator (also spelled Ulaanbaatar), was not very exciting. It contained several Soviet-style buildings, many of which were dilapidated and crumbling. On the outskirts of the capital, like an embrace, you could see hundreds of tents—called "gers" in Mongolia— better known as yurts in the West. Nomads, wanting to escape the hardships of a wandering life, lived in these yurts while they tried to find work in Ulan Bator. More and more Mongolians abandoned their traditional lifestyle to pursue city and factory jobs.

The three national sports are archery, horseback riding, and wrestling. These three games of men date back to ancient times when warlords encouraged competitive sports to toughen up men in readiness for military service. History tells us that they were quite successful in this.

Mongolia produces the best cashmere in the world. It comes from the Zalaa Jinst white goat, the only entirely white breed cashmere goat. These goats live in Mongolia's Gobi Desert—the largest desert in Asia. Our hosts arranged for us to visit the Gobi and spend a night in a yurt. On a fine sunny day, we left Ulan Bator for the Gobi. Our group filled most of the small plane, but there were also other passengers on board. Our guide told us that they were nomads returning to their yurts after shopping in the capital, which explained the presence of hens and goats on board.

As we began flying over the desert, I imagined Genghis Khan and his hordes riding across Asia in their advance westward. These formidable horsemen armed with bows and arrows advanced as far as the outskirts of Vienna, leaving havoc and terror in their wake. They also carried Chinese gunpowder, which they used to lay siege and destroy the cities they encountered. Today, Genghis Khan's portrait appears on currency, vodka bottles, and cigarette packets. His name even graces Ulan Bator's international airport. I thought this to be the equivalent of having Adolf Hitler's image on German currency and his portrait in public places. But in the Mongolian People's Republic, Genghis Khan is a hero.

My daydreaming was interrupted by the view from the window. The land below was diverse. Until then, my idea of a desert was just sand dunes. It was as if some primordial force had scooped out deep ravines, hundreds of ruts, hills, and mountains and placed them haphazardly in this vast wilderness. We were headed for Dalanzadgad, the provincial capital. The pilot announced that we were about to land, but I could not see an airport below, only a single shack in the middle of nowhere with no airstrips or runways. Where was the landing strip? Our pilot began the descent. I saw horses grazing below. The pilot dived fairly low to scatter them, and with the coast clear, our plane landed in the middle of a field close to the shack. It was one of the smoothest landings I have ever experienced. No wonder Mongolian pilots are reputed to be the best in the world.

As we left the aircraft, out of nowhere, a couple of Land Rovers appeared to drive us to our accommodation. There were mountains in the distance, but in front and all around us, I saw only crisscrossing tire marks and deep ruts on the ground.

Our lodgings consisted of a group of yurts set in a circle. One yurt larger than the others was to be our dining room and meeting place. After a traditional Mongolian meal, which included koumis (fermented mare's milk) and offering libations, we settled into our yurts for the night. Suddenly, we heard the unmistakable pitter-patter of rain. It rained all night.

The next morning, we woke up to a miracle. Emerging from our yurt, we were greeted by a rainbow of colors. Flowers everywhere, literally everywhere! The desert had bloomed. It was a magical moment, a patchwork of beautiful colors—thousands of little blooms all rejoicing at their birth. Our guide explained that this rarely occurs. The seeds remain in the ground for years, and the minute the rains come, again, a rare phenomenon: the flowers appear, and the desert explodes with color. I wondered at the tenacity of those seeds that remain hidden underground in permafrost conditions, and then, with the first rain, they break through the ground and greet the sky. Just as some humans rise up and flourish after years of hardship. They lie low, waiting for the right conditions to blossom.

After breakfast, we climbed back into the same Land Rovers as the day before. The previous day's airplane landing was a lot smoother than the jeep ride. The uneven terrain played havoc with my suspension––and I mean mine. I did not care what it did to the Land Rover. We bounced around like ping-pong balls on a jet stream. We were given a guided tour of the greatest desert in Asia. We encountered a huge yak who appeared to eye us, not in a friendly way. We were trespassers. Vultures and other birds of prey circled above, and the guide explained that, most likely, there was a carrion below. His explanation gave me goosebumps. As long as they did not consider us carrion.

The Gobi was impressive, and the variety of scenery was breathtaking. After a short ride, we came to the sand dunes. We left the jeep and wandered about on foot. Suddenly, I found myself separated from the group, all alone in that wilderness. I saw tiny hoof marks in the sand, and I thought: *a small gazelle or rabbit came by*. But no animal was in sight. The isolation was eerie. Silence engulfed me, and suddenly, a strange feeling came over me. I cannot explain it to this day, but it was a mix of fear, foreboding, and utter loneliness. The sound of silence gripped my soul. I felt utter isolation. I was nowhere. This was nowhere. Nowhere was scary. *I am here all alone. I can get lost in this wilderness, and no one will find me. Even my footprints have disappeared in the sand.* It was inexplicable but deeply real and I felt it to my bones. Not only was the silence eerie but there was no wind. It was as if Nature held her breath.

To my great relief, I heard voices approaching as other members of our group started getting closer. Once again, I felt safe. That was the only time when I experienced that kind of dread. I am a city girl through and through—a few moments in the world's most impressive and famous desert scared the heck out of me.

It was time to get back to camp, pack, and head for the airport— the single shack with no runways in the middle of nowhere. As we headed there, our guide made a detour, and suddenly, another shack came into view with "DUTY FREE" painted on it. It was too incongruous for words. There we were, in the middle of the great Gobi desert, and this one shack was trying to attract tourists to buy duty-free goods. We spent some time looking around, and of course, I have to admit that I could not resist a beautiful fur coat with a gorgeous silk lining. It served me well during the cold London winters until I gave it away many years later.

Back in our jeeps, with our duty-free purchases, we headed once again for the airport. As we neared, we saw an aircraft taking off.

" Oh look, that's our airplane, and it's leaving us behind," I chirped jokingly.

"That's not funny!" said one of the group.

Glancing at our guide, I saw consternation on his face. He dashed into the shack, and a heated conversation ensued between him and the only other person there. He returned and admitted that, indeed, our plane had taken off without us, and the next flight would be the following day.

Under normal circumstances, when you miss a flight, you catch the next available flight. But these were not normal circumstances. This was a group of VIPs, guests of the Mongolian government, left stranded in the wilderness. Aware of this, our guide went back into the shack and, after what seemed to be a long time, returned to announce that the plane had been ordered back to pick us up. And that is exactly what happened. As we boarded the aircraft, the look of astonishment and amazement on the faces of the other passengers was obvious. We were equally surprised that the plane had come back for us. To this day, whenever I think of that episode, I chuckle. I have flown over Mongolia many times since but never revisited the steppes, and no plane has ever turned back for me.

***

We now had entered a new phase in our life. We had become empty nesters. It seemed so sudden and strange. I don't think many parents are fully prepared for the empty nest phase. It creeps up on you––or so it seemed to me. I woke up one morning, and the house felt empty and lonely. Gone were the noise, the frantic search for school bags gym clothes, checking the rota for the school run, the PTA meetings, the rearranged timetables, and all the activities surrounding our boys. I missed not having to balance my timetable with that of the children. Iain was in Japan on a scholarship for his PhD, and Alistair was in his final year in college. It was a new normal, but it did not *feel* normal.

I was teaching full-time at Shiplake College and adding to my qualifications. Oxford University offered a Certificate in Teaching English as a Foreign Language (TEFL), and I took it. Later, this would prove to be very useful.

***

In 1990, after 25 years of marriage, Alan and I became another divorce statistic. Being single again was a new ball game for me. The adage: "You know who your friends are when the chips are down," was true in my case, too. Maeve, an Irish friend who used to come by every Saturday and sit at my kitchen table recounting her problems, vanished. She still lived down the road but, for some reason, could not find the time to visit anymore. Perhaps her problems had been resolved, and she no longer needed to talk about them. Another couple, the Armenians, with whom we used to go swimming at the local pool and shared many dinners in each other's homes, also vanished.

But my friend Anna stepped into the breach. She was amazing, kind, thoughtful and supportive. She knocked on my door one day and invited me to her square dance group. She wouldn't take no for an answer.

Living in the suburbs as a single woman was not easy. I did not need to see Alan, now my "ex," arm-in-arm with his new woman in my neighborhood or local store. He had announced to all our former colleagues and friends that he had detached himself from me and attached himself to someone else. I decided to move to London.

Anna and Mum came to help me move. This first attempt at downsizing took time and effort. I organized four big plastic trash bags: one for donations, one for discards, one for selling, and one for stuff to keep. I can't remember how many I filled. I had to move quickly as the house buyers were knocking on the door. I had to be ruthless with the discards and not be ruled by sentiment. My mother protested that I was getting rid of too much stuff. After the move, I discovered that Mum and Anna had surreptitiously repacked many of the discarded items. For some reason, they felt that I still needed to have two of everything—coffee and tea sets and a variety of other paraphernalia.

Life in the metropolis suited me better. I still had bills to pay, as well as a mortgage, so I needed to work. In the next few years, I worked at several jobs. The job market had changed, and short-term contracts were the order of the day, including teaching. Employers preferred to hire and fire people as needed. This meant that they did not have to offer benefits like pensions, sick leave, or holidays. In the early 1990s, there was also an economic recession. Many homeowners found themselves in negative equity as house prices plummeted. Jobs, once considered safe, became less secure and even phased out. The age of computers and digital technology had arrived. Unemployment was on the rise.

My first job in London was with Kensington Temple, a large Pentecostal Church better known as KT. It is in Notting Hill, a part of London I love, and where the movie *Notting Hill,* starring Julia Roberts, was filmed. The first time I called the church to ask for directions, the receptionist said, "On Sunday morning, come to Notting Hill underground station and just follow the crowds." And so it was. As we poured out of the Tube—another name for the London Underground system—up the escalators and into the street, it seemed as if most of that humanity was headed towards KT. It boasted a membership of 5,000 consisting of 110 nationalities. The senior pastor, Colin Dye, often described us as Licorice All Sorts. He was born in Kenya and had been a ballet dancer before he changed direction. I call it a leap of faith. On a few occasions, to highlight a point in his preaching, he would do a high kick to our delight.

I first joined the church as a volunteer but soon was given paid work, thanks largely to Pastor RuthAnn Cannings, who was in charge of the Pastoral Care Office. It was the first time I had come across a female pastor, and I wanted to know more. At the time, the Church of England (CofE) was considering the ordination of women. The very thought caused many Anglicans, both ordained and laymen, to leave the CofE in protest. Heaven forbid that they would have to answer to a female priest, and if heaven did not forbid it, then they would leave. Pentecostals had no such qualms. RuthAnn asked about my training and background.

"I am a bit of a Jack of all trades," I told her.

She laughed. She had a deep, throaty laugh, and her eyes sparkled.

"We can use you," she said. "Let me talk to Rev.Colin Dye."

In no time, RuthAnn came back with the idea of helping the many, mostly young, unemployed members of the congregation.

"You've taught business studies and communication," she said. "A lot of our young people have been out of work for some time. They need to work. They *want* to work. They feel discouraged after so many refusals and disappointments. They need something that will give them confidence and help them believe in themselves."

"I see... It would involve not just skills, but also building up their confidence and self-esteem to help them return to the world of work."

"Exactly," she said.

I had a lot of work ahead of me. The national unemployment figures were reaching new high levels, and our members were included in these statistics. It was RuthAnn's idea to call the series of workshops I put together *Break Free,* and that is how I came to my first job after moving to London. I planned a series of workshops that included a lot of how-to's—how to write a résumé, how to get that job interview, how to overcome disappointment, how to enquire after a particular job advertisement, how to prepare for an interview, how to follow up, how to negotiate a salary. It was quite successful, as many people who attended my workshops found work.

Technically, RuthAnn was my boss. I found her a fascinating person. She was kind and thoughtful and an excellent pastor. I wanted to know more about her. Over the years, we have kept in touch and remained friends. She was born in British Guyana, in South America, and studied nursing in London. For twelve years, she was the private nurse of the famous cellist Jacqueline du Pre, who was stricken with MS at the height of her career. When Jacqueline first met RuthAnn, she immediately nicknamed her "Smiley," and I understand the reason. Daniel Barenboim, du Pre's husband, hired RuthAnn, who became more than a nurse but also an invaluable member of the household. After Jacqueline's death, the press laid siege to RuthAnn's house to feed their insatiable appetite for gossip. It is to RuthAnn's credit that she never gave a single interview or countenanced their pressures for the inside story. To this day, she remains loyal to Daniel Barenboim and Jacqueline du Pre's memory.

I was employed by KT for a year, with the understanding that we would try to get government funding for my workshops. Unfortunately, this did not happen. There was another group doing the same type of work in the area, and despite my many letters and applications, my contract came to an end. Another door was about to open.

The next job was very similar to that at KT. Britain, with its welfare system, takes care of those in need, but the system also encourages abuse and a sense of entitlement. To get people back to work, the government-funded "Back to Work" workshops. It withheld benefits until the unemployed had completed one of these courses. The workshops were geared to different age groups. The first one I taught was for young people. Many were school dropouts whose own parents probably were also jobless and living on benefits. By the mid-90s, it was not uncommon to see second, and third-generation unemployed persons who had never worked. They profited from the welfare system and enjoyed free housing, medical care, and education, among other things.

For some, it became a lifestyle, and they exploited the system. It was becoming endemic.

Being forced by the government to attend these workshops did not suit professional freeloaders. They came to our workshop angry and resentful. The five-day workshops interfered with their routine, whatever that was since they had to be punctual and attend every day. We gave them one-to-one help, interviewed them to find out what skills they had or needed, and assisted them in looking for work. Their language, to say the least, was often colorful.

"F...ing 'ell. Just sign me orf, and I'll be outta here!"

"Sorry, we can't do this. You know you're supposed to be here for the week. It's only five days. And it'll help you get a job."

"I don't want a f...ing job."

At least they were honest and made their intentions clear. It was impossible to reason or argue with the unreasonable. I remember one 17-year-old mother saying: "I'll bloody well go and 'ave another f....ing kid if they make me go to work." She had no intention of joining the workforce, preferring to stay home and have one kid after another, with fathers unknown. She received child benefits for every kid she produced. So the more kids, the more money.

My co-worker, Mark, was an ex-army Taekwondo black belt champion. Once or twice, he had to escort or restrain the occasional troublemaker. Strangely enough, by the end of the week, many of those who completed the course thanked us and said they were glad they had stayed and had found it helpful. They even wrote—those who could write—comments full of praise for our teaching.

After that, I also worked for another "Back to Work" government-funded course. This one was for executives who had been out of work for some time. There was no time limit on attendance, and most of them were men in their mid-forties to late fifties—CEOs, bank managers, and management bosses. They had no idea how to go about looking for work. They had been hired through the *old boys'* network or worked their way up over the years. They had held their positions for a couple of decades and suddenly found themselves let go. The job market had changed drastically, and they had not caught up with the changes. For years, they had relied on their secretaries or PAs to take dictation, write their letters, correct their spelling, answer the phone, make their appointments, fend off unwanted calls, and keep their diaries, both business and personal. Many did not know how to use a word processor or computer. They could not type. That was the secretary's job.

We had one client who always turned up early. He waited patiently by the front door each morning, come rain or shine. He was a former banker and CEO. We wondered why he was always the first on the doorstep.

"Mr. Jones. We don't open until ten. You don't have to come so early."

"It's alright. I don't mind," he'd say.

"But it's freezing cold. You don't have to stand out in the rain and snow."

"It's OK. I don't mind."

Nothing persuaded him to come at 10 am. We discovered the reason later. Apparently, he was ashamed of being let go. His wife colluded with him. Each morning, at the same time, he left the house in his business suit with a briefcase—as he had done for many years—boarded the train, and arrived outside our premises an hour early. The briefcase contained his sandwiches. We had to teach him how to use the word processor and write a resumé. We never found out whether he ever got a job again.

Following that, I did some temporary work. Through contacts, I obtained part-time work teaching communications and customer relations at the West London Vocational College. One of the classes consisted of difficult adolescents who resented being there. Many of them, school dropouts, were forced to attend college or else they could not claim benefits. They were grumpy. They turned up late and paid no attention in class. I gave them several warnings, to no avail.

It would have been easy for me to say nothing, pretend to teach them, and let them be. But this class had no intention of learning anything. I came to a decision. One morning, after they had all dragged themselves in, in dribs and drabs, I said: "I have an important announcement today. Please listen carefully. I am not in the habit of taking money under false pretenses. None of you is prepared to buckle down and learn or work. You are not interested in learning, and I am not interested in teaching you. I can't teach you. I don't want to waste my time or yours. I am resigning from this class. Goodbye!" They all sat there speechless. You could hear a pin drop as I walked out, never to return. There was no comeback from the college either. I think they knew no one else wanted to teach that particular group.

Years later, I met one of those students, and she said to me: "Aw, Miss, you were the best teacher. We never got another teacher like you after you left us. I wish you 'aden't gone."

I couldn't help but smile. Today, every time I recount this particular episode to my teacher friends, they tell me that, at times, they, too, wish they could drop certain classes.

***

Like most people, I recall where I was on September 11, 2001. In 1999, I started working at Southbank International School in London. The students attending were the scions of foreign diplomats, businessmen, and parents who wanted their children to graduate with an International Baccalaureate qualification. I had great colleagues, and Ruth, my department head, and I soon became close friends. Like me, she had traveled extensively and lived abroad. She was also efficient, and the ESL (English as a Second Language) Department worked extremely well under her. I worked there for a couple of years. One day, I was in the staff room when Beverly, the American music teacher, burst in shouting: "The Twin Towers are under attack. They are down! Something's happened."

I wasn't quite sure what or where the Twin Towers were. Then another colleague came in and said: "Quick! Turn on the TV. Something terrible's happened in New York!"

We did, and there it was: the by now all too familiar and infamous picture of the Twin Towers under attack as the commandeered airplanes flew into them. We stood there motionless for a few minutes, unable to take it in. Lessons were canceled, and TV monitors in every classroom were turned on. Students and teachers alike looked on in bewilderment and shock. It was a terrible sight. Back then, we did not have or even know the expression "lock-down," but the principal locked the doors. The phone calls started—anxious parents calling to ask if their kids were safe and telling us they were on their way to pick them up. In the weeks that followed, a group of us went to the American Embassy and signed the condolence book. After that, we put security locks on the doors and installed an entry phone system that monitored people coming in and going out. The entire world had changed.

***

I had signed up with an employment agency, and I was hardly ever without work. My jobs were all short-term contracts. Some were interesting and some not, but at least I could pay my bills. Life in London was never boring. There was so much to do and see. My home was centrally located and close to museums, art galleries, and the West End, with its many theaters.

I took classes in Chinese Brush Painting at the Mary Ward Centre and rekindled my love and interest in this ancient art form. I founded the London branch of the Chinese Brush Painting Association and was its first president. It is still active and flourishing to this day.

There was no shortage of things to do or see. My younger son, Alistair, was living with me, and his older brother, Iain, had finished his PhD at the University of Electricity in Tokyo. Life was good, but it was time for a change. I wanted to pay off my mortgage as all my equity was tied up in my London home. I was getting older and did not want to have debt hanging over me. I needed to be financially secure. Part-time jobs and short-term contracts did not guarantee security or tenure. I was tired of going from job to job and waiting for the agency to call.

It was at this time that I met Caroline during an evening service at my church in Central London. We started talking, and she told me that she was working as a translator in Beijing. That's when I had an "aha" moment. It was more than "aha" it was an epiphany. *Won't it be fun and exciting to get a job in China? I can let my London house and work overseas for a few years. I have the qualifications, and I know something about Chinese customs. I know how to use chopsticks. I can also continue studying Chinese brush painting.* That was it! I, too, could try to get a job in China.

My "aha" moment came just at the right time. China had been nominated to host the 2008 Summer Olympics. English language learning was exploding all over Cathay. In no time, I enlisted with a British company sending EFL teachers there. I chose Beijing, the capital of northern China. I was ready for China. I hoped that China was ready for me.

It was not a slow boat that took me there, but a fast jet, fueled by my financial needs, China's need for EFL teachers, and its desire to impress the world with a great Olympics spectacle.

CHAPTER FIVE

CHINA

After winning its bid to host the 2008 Summer Olympics, China's communist government mandated that all Chinese working in the tourist business learn English, from barkeepers to restaurant waiters, from taxi drivers to tour guides. When the communist government issues a diktat, everyone obeys. Jobs in the capital, especially in the tourist trade, are much sought after and not easy to come by.

On my flight to China, I sat next to a young German who told me he was going to teach English "somewhere in China." He spoke with a heavy German accent, and his grammar was sketchy, but he was upbeat and excited. We were part of an influx of English teachers pouring into the Middle Kingdom to teach in schools, universities, colleges, and other establishments.

When I arrived in Beijing in early January, snow covered the city. I was about to experience the first of several winters—a time when bone-freezing, icy winds blow south from Siberia through the Mongolian steppes. My company put me up in a small hotel in West Beijing until I could find a suitable apartment.

It was different from China, which I had known in the 70s when I lived in Hong Kong. At that time, China was closed to foreign journalists and tourists. After Mao died in 1976, the bamboo curtain gradually came down. By the time I got there in 2001, Mao was referred to as the "Red Emperor." The Chinese now claimed that his rule had been correct 70 percent of the time and wrong 30 percent of the time. If it had been up to me, I would have reversed those percentages, and even that would have been too generous. No one mentioned the other 30 percent—the excesses of the Cultural Revolution, the suppression of the democracy movement, or the Tiananmen Square massacre in 1989. I knew better than to allude to them.

Before I left England, I had warned friends not to mention religion or politics in their communications. I knew it was highly likely that they—whoever "they" might be— would eavesdrop or check most of my emails and phone calls. I was not paranoid, but I suspected that my new apartment might be bugged. I had nothing to hide. But when you live in a communist country, rules differ dramatically from those in a Western democracy. Despite reforms and changes instituted by Deng Xiaoping with the opening of China, the communist party still kept tight control over great swathes of people's lives.

The maxim "To get rich is glorious," attributed to Deng, had unshackled the economy and freed the people to amass wealth. However, the country was still run by an authoritarian Communist regime. Getting rich was okay since rich people also enriched China, but meddling in politics or criticizing the regime was not okay.

All these thoughts buzzed through my head as I came out of my hotel that first cold and frosty morning. New smells, noises, and sights added to my exhilaration. I felt like Alice in Wonderland, and the snow added to the feeling. The sidewalks had been salted and sanded. Still, I walked carefully, each step crunching the snow under my feet.

My thoughts were soon interrupted, aware that I was being followed. In the beginning, it was just a feeling. I crossed the street, and so did he. I turned left, and so did he. I turned right, and so did he. As I turned right again, I caught a glimpse of the man behind me. He was fairly tall and wearing a rather drab, dirty raincoat. It looked well-padded. *How can I shake him off? I need to get rid of him.* The faster I walked or crossed a street, the more he kept up with me and getting closer. He started to say something, too, but as I did not speak Mandarin, I had no idea what he wanted. Another thought crossed my mind: *A man wearing a dirty white coat... Bummer! I've come all this way to be accosted by a flasher! How can I lose him?"* I kept walking and thinking: *of all the places, of all the cities, I come to China to meet a man in sub-zero temperatures who is determined to show me his frigid digit.*

Somehow, from the bottomless reservoir of memory, I remembered some advice from years ago: *If you meet a flasher, you must not show shock, fear, or embarrassment. That is what they want. Just make some kind of disparaging remark and show you are not impressed.* Since I could not make disparaging remarks in Chinese, I decided to laugh disparagingly—whatever that was—to show that I was not embarrassed or frightened.

I turned round to confront him. And, as I had feared, he immediately opened his raincoat. Inside was a veritable shop of DVDs, and he was saying: "DVD, DVD, You buy! You buy! DVD." Several pockets inside his coat bulged with CDs and DVDs. I burst out laughing with relief. In retrospect, I don't think I could have managed a disparaging laugh.

I learned later that the illegal reproduction of movies and music is a thriving industry in China. My stalker in the padded raincoat was one of hundreds of sellers I encountered during my time there. They knew the watering holes foreigners frequented, and they came to our table to sell their DVDs. If we showed interest, a fellow co-conspirator lurking in the background arrived with more goods. They had American, French, Russian, Chinese, Japanese, British and Australian movies. If they did not carry something we wanted, they would get it for us. They would even bring it up to our apartment. Some of the movies were available even before they were released in their country of origin. Most of the time, the quality was good, and the price was around five to eight dollars. By the time I left Beijing three years later, I had amassed around 350 DVDs, which I shipped back home. I purchased them from the official government shops but was refused a receipt when I asked for one detailing the items. China uses the PAL system, so any DVDs purchased there will be played in the UK, Australia, and any country with the same system.

Many of these purveyors of pirated copies were "illegals," or at least that's how we referred to them. They had come from the countryside and the far-flung reaches of China to find work in the cities. Life among the rice paddy fields at the subsistence level may seem appealing to romantics, armchair visionaries, and others who have never experienced the reality of harsh winters or famine. Under the Hukou system, the government tried to contain migration to the cities and prevent the depletion of labor from agricultural areas. However, the preparations for the Olympics created opportunities for work in most urban areas. Migrant workers poured into big cities like Beijing, Shanghai, Chengdu, and Guangdong, looking for work. They were part of the black economy and subsisted working in construction, kitchens, selling pirated DVDs, or any other work they could find.

With the Olympics looming, Beijing was undergoing the mother of all facelifts at a frenetic pace. Big cities are noisy anyway, but the constant pounding of jackhammers and drills reminded us, day and night, that China intended to impress the world and show off how far it had advanced. It had, indeed, come a long way since the days of drab uniforms and Mao-style boiler suits and famines. China was determined to show the world that the dragon was awake and on the move. It still described itself as a developing country with a developing economy, but it was about to take a giant leap to superpower.

My British friend, Julie, who is married to a local man, said to me one day: "My mother-in-law is of two minds about the coming games."

"Why? I thought all Beijingers welcome the chance to show off their city to the rest of the world."

"Her house is along one of the official routes to the Olympic Village, and the government painted all the buildings, including hers, to make them look like new."

"Well then, that's good, isn't it?" I said.

"They painted only the front of her house, so the sides and back look shabbier than ever. She asked them to paint the whole house, but they refused."

This got me wondering whether the Games were going to be a façade and whether the real China would remain out of sight. As we witnessed the preparations, my friends and I joked: "See that bridge and overhead roads above? They weren't there yesterday."

The effort was massive, the kind of effort that could only be put together by a country with a strong central government and millions of laborers, planners, and designers. It was all hands on deck for the glory of China. Starbucks, McDonalds, and pizza parlors spread everywhere like measles. There was even a Starbucks kiosk inside the Forbidden City. It was incongruous. I wondered, *How can the country of tea host a Starbucks inside one of its most revered ancient monuments?* When I revisited China in 2011, the coffee shop had been removed. Wise decision. The ancestors can now rest in peace.

Unfortunately, in its efforts to modernize and impress the world, the government destroyed many ancient and beautiful buildings. Entire communities were removed to make room for the new. Concrete Goliath-size blocks of glass and steel stretched into the sky like monoliths of a new age, altering the entire Beijing skyline. The Government, hell-bent on rivaling and even surpassing the West in impressive modern architecture, bulldozed away centuries of history. It continues to this day. I could see before my very own eyes the fulfillment of Mao's dictum: *"Before construction, we must have destruction."*

Beijing, Shanghai, and most major cities quickly became like other big cities around the world, with the same franchises, corporate offices, and shopping malls.

To the consternation of many, the quaint old Hutong households, where generations had lived, were disappearing. The history of entire communities vanished under concrete. I had some interesting discussions with my friend Tommy Wu on this.

"Tommy, Beijing is losing its unique character, becoming just like any other city in the West. What do you think?"

"I know, it's a shame," he said, "but the young people like it. We have a new middle class, and frankly, we've never had it so good. A few years ago, we had nothing, only poverty and famine."

"But, can't you have progress without destroying so much of your patrimony and history?"

"It's not easy," he replied. "After years of humiliating treaties, gun-war diplomacy, and feudal wars, we are in a hurry to move on."

His command of English was excellent, and conversing with him was easy and interesting. I realized I had no right to tell the Chinese people to slow down. In the West, too, we had destroyed a great deal through our so-called advance. To this day, we continue to damage our environment and cause massive pollution.

"I hope you learn from our mistakes and don't repeat them," I told him. "I can foresee a time when China will become the world's leading economy. It is to its credit that it has managed to drag its people out of dire poverty and feed, house, and clothe millions without a revolution."

Tommy was thoughtful, "Well... we did have the Cultural Revolution that delayed things. I'm sure if it hadn't happened, we would be much further ahead. Time will tell."

In the meantime, I loved wandering around those narrow Hutong alleys, away from the touristy areas, where life continued at a less frantic pace. Even the jackhammer drills seemed quieter there. I caught glimpses of courtyards through half-open doors and imagined generations of families living together. Through doors left ajar, I saw children playing, women cooking over charcoal stoves, laughter, noisy chatter, bowls of steaming rice, and heard the clacking of mahjong tiles. I saw crickets and small birds kept in bamboo cages. These were their pets. Canines were kept as guard dogs.

There was a pecking order inside the siheyuan—the best rooms on the ground floor were reserved for the oldest, more venerated family members. From there, like tentacles, spread the living quarters of sons, in-laws, uncles, and cousins. Men took precedence over women and wives over concubines and servants. At least in theory.

***

Within weeks of my arrival, by happy accident, I found a new job, changed my apartment, and trebled my salary. It was serendipitous. Caroline, the friend who first told me about jobs in China, visited me soon after I arrived in Beijing. She was one of the English editors on the *China Daily* newspaper. She corrected and edited copies submitted by Chinese writers. I asked her which church she attended.

"I go to the Christian Fellowship in the Chaoyang district," she said. "It's at the 21st Century Hotel. It's for expats."

"What do you mean it's for expats?"

"It's only for foreigners. The Chinese can't go there. You have to show your passport at the door," she said.

"But why aren't the Chinese allowed to go there?"

"The Chinese Christians go to the designated churches, which the Government officially approves. Most Chinese believers attend the underground church."

"Oh, I see," I said. I didn't really "see" or understand. I made a mental note to find out later. I was still jet-lagged from my trip. "So why is it called the 21st-century hotel?"

"Because it *is* a hotel. They have a huge auditorium and each Sunday, the Christian Fellowship fills it to the brim. It's non-denominational and all the services are in English. See you there this Sunday, and remember to bring your passport."

"I'd think my face is my passport. I can't pass for Chinese."

"All the same, bring your passport. It's the rule and we don't want to upset the authorities. They could close us down."

She had been in China a couple of years and knew the ropes. I had a lot to learn. I followed her advice and made the 21st Century Hotel my church also, showing my passport at the door, like everyone else.

A few weeks later, early in the morning, I received a phone call.

"Nora, this is Nick. Remember, we met in church and you visited my school?"

Nick was the principal of one of the international schools in Beijing. I had met him and his wife in church a couple of weeks earlier. "Yes, how are you?"

"I have a favor to ask you. I'm in a bit of a jam. It's quite a problem actually, and I thought you might be able to help. You said you are a qualified teacher?"

"Yes, I am. I taught at the American International School in London."

"Well, my English teacher has just walked out. I need an English teacher for the High School by Monday."

"Oh, I'm sorry to hear it. How can I help?"

"Can you come and work for us?" he said.

"I don't know. I have to ask my boss if he'll release me from my contract. This is Thursday, and you said you need someone by this coming Monday?"

"Yes, that's right. I have no one else. We must have someone qualified, like you."

"I'll see what I can do and let you know." I hung up.

Alex, my boss and owner of the language school, realized he could not match the salary or benefits offered by the international school, so he released me from my contract. That's how I came to treble my salary, just a few weeks after landing in Beijing. I also moved into a more central and comfortable apartment. The school arranged for me to obtain the much-coveted "Z" visa, which allowed freedom of movement to expats working in China.

The international school, like the church, was for foreign nationals only. Chinese citizens could not enroll their children. Teaching was bilingual in the elementary school. Lessons were taught in both Mandarin and English—a good model for bi-lingual and bi-cultural education. The foreign staff came from Australia, Canada, and Britain. The student's parents were diplomats, foreign business people, or overseas Chinese who held foreign passports. We had a few Korean students whose parents worked for major Korean companies like LG, Samsung, and Hyundai.

Dating back to the days of Confucius, education and learning are held in high esteem in China. Teachers are valued and respected. Over many centuries, the Imperial Examination system created a meritocracy. Whenever I mentioned I was a teacher people showed their approval, saying: "Ah. A teacher, you are very clever." Apparently, they believed that you have to be clever to be a teacher.

"Thank you for coming to China. You are so brave to leave your country and come to teach us. Thank you," they said with deep bows.

This attitude toward teaching, coupled with China's insatiable desire to learn English, created the perfect atmosphere for expat teachers of English. It was such a welcome change from the rowdy and often undisciplined mob I dealt with in England.

However, because of the elevated status of teachers, great results are also expected. In Korea, parents threaten their naughty children that they will inform the teacher of their misdemeanors. In Korean culture, it's the teacher's job to punish the miscreants—even with corporal punishment.

Teachers are also expected to be available to parents at all hours. One particular Korean boy in my class was disruptive. I sent a note to his parents, and the father came to see me. "I'm afraid your son is not a good student, Mr. Kim. I often have to send him out of the class, as he causes a disturbance." The father agreed with me.

"Oh, I know. You must discipline him. Beat him up, like I do."

"Mr. Kim. Your son is over six feet tall" *and weighs twice my weight.* "This is an international school. We do not mete out corporal punishment to our students."

"Well, you should. He needs it, and he deserves it. It's your job."

"No, Mr. Kim. My job is to *teach* your son. *Your* job is to discipline him. We don't beat our students."

"Well, how do you expect them to obey then?" he asked.

"By following our rules and instructions. This is how we do things in an international school." He was not happy with my answer. Soon after, the principal expelled the boy. That was not my only run-in with an ambitious parent.

During a parent-teacher conference, another Korean parent accosted me. She came straight to the point."I want you to give my daughter more homework and lessons during the summer vacation."

"I'm sorry, I am not in Beijing during the holidays."

"You can email her the lessons," the mother said.

"I see. But who is going to mark the papers?"

"You will, of course. I'll email them back to you," she promised.

"Sorry, Mrs. Lee, I can't do that. I need my holiday too. I am in school from seven in the morning each day and leave at seven in the evening. After that, my time is my own. I need time to rest, relax, and play. That way, I can be a better teacher, not only for your daughter but for all my other students."

"But my daughter needs..."

"What your daughter needs is to have more free time herself and be allowed to be a child, to play with her friends, and not be overburdened with extra lessons and classes."

Once again, I had to deal with a parent who could not understand that teachers have a life outside the classroom. She, too, needed a lesson in Piaget instead of Confucius. She was typical of most Asian parents who have exceedingly high aspirations for their children.

I met the principal in the school courtyard one day. "How's the football team going, Nick?"

He looked at me and sighed: "I can't get the little blighters to come."

"Why? I thought you organized it after school hours and gave it a lot of publicity."

"It's the f...ing parents." An Australian, he did not mince his words. Down Under, sports is like a religion, and Nick used to be a sports teacher. He was trying very hard to form a soccer team, but most parents did not share his passion. They were either too busy in their own jobs or busy taking their kids to extra-curricular activities. They focused entirely on academic achievement. The onus was on the school and teachers to meet these often unattainable goals.

I heard stories of teachers who had failed a student or had given them low grades, only to find that the low marks had been *upgraded* by the administration. I asked my friend Imelda the reason.

"In China, face is everything. You can't lose face. If students get low grades, it's a poor reflection on the school and its teaching."

"But if the students deserved these low grades...? "

"Chinese teachers don't give low grades, as it reflects badly on themselves. The *teachers* lose face."

I was learning the importance of "face" in China. The loss of face can result in fights, revenge killings even blood feuds that last for years.

Plagiarism was also okay. Students lifted entire passages from the internet and included them in their essays without so much as a reference. As one Chinese friend told me, "It's okay to cheat your way to the top."

When the social pyramid is so big—very broad at the base, and the top very far away— clawing your way up, by any means, is considered something of a feat. Even youngsters knew how to grab every chance they got for self-improvement. Thousands of school kids in Beijing consider me, and every Western tourist, a free and available source of English lessons. Each time I ventured out of my apartment, I was accompanied by young people who wanted to engage in English conversation.

Mandarin Chinese is not easy to learn. It is tonal, and if you hit the wrong syllable, you might say something unintended. I also learned that certain words carry superstitious beliefs. The Chinese word for the number four sounds like "sir." But if you hit the wrong tone it means death, and that is considered bad luck. For this reason, the number four is avoided. Often, in multi-story buildings, there is no mention of a fourth floor. By contrast, number eight is considered lucky. Bribes are paid to get a house number, telephone number, or car registration with as many number eights as possible. My apartment was, in fact on the fourth floor, but listed as being on the fifth floor. The elevator button went from 3 to 5. Four did not exist. It was weird. I existed. My apartment existed. But my floor did not exist. Another China experience.

The concept of one's own space is absent in China. In cities people literally live cheek-to-jowl. If you politely stand by a doorway to let another person through, you wait for an eternity. All humanity will walk by, without a second thought. I soon learned not to hold doors open for anyone. Exiting an elevator was equally difficult—whenever I tried to get out, another lot entered. It was not long before I realized that the only way to exit was to push my way through the bodies. I learned to use my elbows to great effect when negotiating exits and entryways.

One of the first Chinese words I learned was "How much does it cost?" followed by, "Oh no, it's too expensive!" I must have managed this very well, because my Chinese friends, and colleagues, wanted to shop with me.

There are three prices in China: one for locals—the lowest price––one for overseas Chinese, and one for tourists. I always aimed for the lowest price. "Nora, we want to come shopping with you. You always get the best prices. Even better than us. How do you do it?" my friends asked.

"I never want it so badly that I can't walk away from it. That's the secret." It remains my motto to date.

Bargaining over the price of anything in China is an art form. In fact, it is expected. Doing business in the Far East has its own rules. Most business is conducted over a meal, which, sometimes, can include a multi-course banquet. The word used is "panyio" which means friend. You become "friends" after several bouts of haggling. Then, you clinch the deal. Bargaining back and forth is necessary since both seller and buyer need to save face.

***

I had several overseas visitors during my time in China. Word got around that I had a modern two-bedroom apartment in central Beijing and guests were welcome. "Modern" meant that I had a fully equipped kitchen with an oven. It also meant that I had a Western-style bathroom. At that time, the authorities were building modern conveniences around Beijing. In fact, there were two types of public restrooms: Western and Chinese. The Chinese-style restrooms were latrine-type squats. I asked my friend why the two different types. "We don't like to sit on the seat. We think it's sitting on someone else's urine or shit. Squatting is more hygienic," she said.

"What if someone is elderly and can't squat?"

"We are used to squatting from childhood. If people can't squat then we help them."

That's true communal living, I thought, *I wouldn't want someone to wipe my derrière, if I can't do the squats anymore."*

Whenever I needed to visit the bathroom away from home, I dived into the nearest five-star hotel, (luxury hotels were also being built at high speed all over China) and spent my penny in comfort. Actually it wasn't a penny but a Chinese Renminbi, China's currency, which translates as "people's money." I was comfortable spending the people's money in the toilet of a five-star hotel.

***

Since I had gone to China to pay off my mortgage, I have worked two jobs during my time there. Along with teaching, I worked for the British Council. It was serendipity. An English colleague asked me if I wanted to be an IELTS examiner.

"What's that? I asked. "I've never heard of it."

"It stands for International English Language Testing System. Cambridge University developed it. It's an international standardized test of English language proficiency. The British Council runs it. We need more examiners, and I thought of you."

"How does it work?"

"When the Chinese apply to go overseas for work or study, they have to show proficiency in English. They sit the IELTS test. If they fail, they can't get a visa."

"I already have a job, and it would be difficult for me to get away," I said.

"The oral tests are always held at the weekend. The British Council will train you. They set up everything. They fly us to various parts of China, put us up in first-class hotels, and hold the tests during the day. Evenings are free, and we have great fun exploring new places. We fly back to Beijing on Sunday afternoon."

And that is how I ended up working two jobs in China. On Friday, I arrived at school with a small carry-on, and, after the last class, caught a cab to the airport where I met my other IELTS colleagues.

The IELTS training by the British Council was something of an eye-opener. It consisted mostly of looking out for cheats. The trainer explained to us the many ways the students tried to cheat. Cell phones, wristwatches, writing materials, and bags were not allowed in the exam room. We provided them with mechanical pencils, erasers, and paper. No prior communication with students was permitted. Seemingly draconian precautions, perhaps, but necessary, because our clients were determined to get that visa. A few times, students attempted to bribe me by asking me out for a meal, inviting me to their homes, or offering me some regional food delicacy.

My work with the British Council took me all over China, enabling me to see places and towns outside Beijing. We went to Dalien, Tianjin, Xian, and many other cities. After work, we would wander around town visiting the night markets, sampling local food, and taking in the sights. I enjoyed the work, the travel, the stay in five-star hotels, and the extra money. I also had interesting colleagues. One day, as we were marking written exam papers at the British Council, the Australian colleague sitting across the table introduced herself.

"Hi, my name is Hariklia. I'm from Melbourne." I knew right away that she was Greek. You can't be called "Hariklia" and not be Greek. So, to her great surprise, I responded to her in Greek.

Another colleague was James. His provenance was shrouded in mystery. Some said he was from New Zealand, others from South Africa, but he maintained he was from Britain, and even hinted at having blue blood. He stood at the bar and regaled those present with his exploits. His booming voice ensured that everyone within earshot could hear him. He laughed at his own jokes and was full of braggadocio.

He seemed to have a penchant for Chinese girls. Each time I saw him on the exam circuit he was surrounded by a gaggle of nubile young women. And then he vanished. After a few months, I asked: "Where's James?"

I was told that James no longer worked for the British Council. Months later, the full story emerged. Somehow it became public knowledge that he had been enticing young female students to his hotel room, under the pretext of coaching them for the exam. After his dismissal he went around Beijing asking for money to start his own English Language School—such schools were mushrooming all over China and were very profitable. He promised those funding him that they would become shareholders. After amassing enough funds, James absconded with the money to the Philippines. I can imagine him holding forth at some bar in Manila, boasting of his grand schemes and sexual exploits.

Not all expats were old roués like James. The reasons for living overseas vary from person to person. For me, it was economic, for others perhaps a search for something spiritual. I encountered a few of these seekers, mostly young and usually male, who had come to China to "find themselves." To fill a spiritual void in their lives, they were attracted to China's rich history, culture, and civilization. In their search for Nirvana, some of them embraced everything Chinese, from religion, Confucian teaching, the Taoist "Way," and even attire—long flowing gowns as seen in old Chinese paintings. I felt sorry for them because I knew that the Chinese were laughing at them. The pragmatic and down-to-earth denizens of Cathay knew that no Westerner, however hard they tried, could ever become "Chinese." A Chinese friend, with a wicked sense of humor and perfect English, said: "Their eyes are not slitty enough," and with that, she pulled up the corners of her eyes.

When I began to study and take classes in brush painting I, too, experienced how the Chinese considered their culture unique and exclusive. I sensed they thought, that as a *laowai* I could never master the art of the dancing brush. When I reminded them that the Chinese can master various aspects of Western culture such as classical music, jazz, or painting, they always answered: "We can. We work hard at it and succeed, but foreigners can never excel at anything Chinese, the way *we Chinese* do."

"Why do they try and imitate us?" my friend Elizabeth Tang asked. "There must be something lacking in their culture if they come here to espouse ours."

I had to agree. "We have watered down our own culture and belief system, and many people don't have a sense of belonging. We have created a lost generation that is now seeking something to cling to and espouse as its own."

She looked somewhat puzzled. I continued, "On the other hand, there is something admirable in your culture and civilization. It has survived over the millennia... wars and revolutions unable to destroy it."

She thought for a moment, "I guess our young people have different priorities," she said. "We believe in education. We have a long tradition of learning, beginning with the Imperial Examination System, hard work and study are virtues encouraged by the family and the government."

This reminded me of the many banners and ads often daubed over fading plaster walls, urging the populace to work hard. These exhortations could be found all over the country, in remote towns, hamlets, and villages. "Then why do so many of your young people want to go overseas?" I asked.

"They want to get their Masters or PhDs and obtain knowledge in those areas and subjects that China needs. The government gives them grants and on their return, they are ensured jobs with special privileges."

I thought this sounded like a one-way street. China believed that it could take what it needed from the West for its development and aggrandizement, but was reluctant to share its own specialties and successes with the rest of the world. The Middle Kingdom was good at adopting *and* adapting. Its brand of communism was very different from that of Karl Marx and Lenin. I kept my thoughts to myself, and to Elizabeth I said: "I guess Chinese young people don't have the time to sit around and contemplate their navels."

She laughed: "No, we don't have that luxury. Besides, we have a saying: 'You don't work, you don't eat,' and we certainly need to eat." I admired her down-to-earth attitude.

However, not all teaching and child nurturing centered entirely on materialism. Filial piety is considered a virtue in China. Young people are expected to take care of their elderly, be it parents, grandparents or other senior members of their extended family. During one of my travels, a seven-year-old asked me: "How old are you?"

"Oh I'm very old," I replied.

"Then why are you here?"

"To make money and get rich," I replied.

"But you are a *laowai,* you're already rich."

Like most Chinese, he believed that all Westerners are rich, and came to his country for China's benefit, not the other way round.

"If you are very old, why aren't your children taking care of you?"

I smiled. Even a seven-year-old had learned that it is the duty of the young to take care of the elders in the family. It had already been instilled in him.

CHAPTER SIX

CHINA - VISITORS

When Ruth, my colleague from the American International School in London, visited me in Beijing in 2004, we decided to go on vacation. We had debated whether to holiday in Phuket, Thailand, but ultimately chose Hanoi—a decision more fortuitous than we could have imagined. We were due to fly out the day after Christmas. On that day, the deadliest tsunami in history engulfed several countries in Southeast Asia. Phuket was one of them, and many people died there.

In Vietnam, Ruth and I took a cruise among the magical karsts of Ha Long Bay—an area known for its emerald waters and thousands of towering limestone islands topped by rainforests. It is classified among the new Seven Wonders of Nature and is one of the most beautiful places I have ever visited. It reminded me of Guilin in China, with similar karsts along the Jade River.

The limestone rocky islands conceal many nooks, crannies, and caves. Our guide told us that during the Vietnam War, the Americans bombed the area heavily in their efforts to flush out the Vietcong. "But they never found us," he said. "We were well protected, and the islands were the perfect hideout for us. We have almost 2,000 islands, and they did not know where we were."

He said this with pride—but without rancor. What surprised me during our visit to the country was the absence of any bitterness, anger, or recrimination. The war had happened, Vietnam had won, it was now over, and the country was ready to move on. They envied China to the north, which was making great economic strides. They also feared it.

"We worry. We have a long history of wars and fights with China," he said. "We worry that as they get stronger, they will rekindle their old claims on our territory." He went on to say:

"We have a common border with China, and they keep pushing it southward. At night, we push it back."

This did not surprise me. I was becoming increasingly aware that China would soon flex its muscles and claim hegemony over many nearby islands and countries. China's neighbors were watching the stirring dragon with trepidation.

We asked our guide to direct us to some tourist shops to buy souvenirs. He took us to an open market, where there were many small shops specializing in beautiful handicrafts made by the locals. Many of the artists were handicapped, with terrible deformities, yet they produced wonderful art.

"Why so many disabled people here?" I asked.

"They are the victims of napalm and sarin gas dropped by the Americans," our guide explained. "Some of them are second-generation victims." To this day, it is difficult to describe my horror, shame, and guilt when I saw these victims of chemical warfare.

I find it ironic that years later, in 2019, President Trump chose Hanoi for a summit with Korea's Kim Jong Un. He and his administration must have felt safe holding talks in a country in which the US had used weapons of mass destruction—and where both sides had suffered great losses.

After we visited Vietnam, Ruth and I flew to Harbin, in northeast China, for the annual Ice Festival. One of the most memorable trips I took in China remains engraved in my memory. It is the world's largest and most impressive annual snow and ice festival, with temperatures dropping 31 degrees below freezing. Huge chunks of ice are harvested from the nearby river. Once the ice is in place, sculptors chisel away to create giant masterpieces, including statues of famous people, places, and historic events. The year we attended, the sculptors created nearly full-size replicas of the White House, the Taj Mahal, Big Ben, and the Kremlin. At night, the park and its exhibits are illuminated, creating a phantasmagorical fairyland.

We wandered from building to building—from the White House to Versailles, to St. Peter's, to the Kremlin—all beautifully sculpted in ice. I was so well insulated against the cold that I looked like the Michelin tire man. There were slides, walkways, bridges, and plazas, all made of ice. We often had to stop at food stalls to warm our multi-gloved hands over a brazier and have a hot drink.

In Harbin, we also visited the Snow Leopard and Siberian Tiger Conservation Park. Our guide told us they do not call them "Siberian" but instead "Chinese snow leopards." I thought: Ah, another country bordering China with which China has disputed borders. Siberia was indeed a few miles north of us, and China had not relinquished its claim over it.

While Ruth and I were walking in the streets of Harbin, a Chinese man approached and began to yell at us. He was aggressive, waving his arms and pointing. From my limited repertoire of Chinese words, I worked out that he was saying, "Get out, get out!" Then he spat at Ruth. This was so uncharacteristic, because Chinese men do not explode in public. A small crowd had gathered. We did not know what to make of it, and Ruth said, "What's wrong with him? He's very angry about something."

As soon as he heard her, his whole demeanor changed. He immediately calmed down. A young student standing nearby, who had witnessed the scene, explained that the cantankerous old man thought we were Russian.

"Why does he dislike Russians? They're your neighbors."

"That's the problem," he replied. "We get many Russian women coming over. They earn money as prostitutes. They are in demand by some Chinese men, who prefer them to Chinese girls. We don't like it."

"So why does the government allow it?" I asked.

"They don't. But they don't ban them either. This is illicit business. The women are smuggled across the border. This guy thought you were Russian. I'm sorry for what happened."

The student looked embarrassed by the incident. He felt that we might go away with a bad impression of his country. Ruth is a natural redhead, and many Russian women dye their hair red. I thought it funny and odd to be mistaken for a prostitute.

Oh well, I filed that away as yet another China experience. Years later, in another country, I would be asked by a government official whether I was a prostitute.

***

Another visitor was Toby, my friend from San Francisco. We decided to go to Yunnan province for a holiday. Yunnan is in southwest China and is mostly populated by non-Chinese ethnic minorities.

It was early spring and cold as we left Beijing and flew to Kunming, the Yunnan capital. At our hotel, we ordered a cooked breakfast. When it arrived, Toby said, "Look! Look at my plate!"

I looked at hers and then at mine. Our cooked breakfast was floating on a bed of coagulated bacon fat. It was that cold! Even our breath was visible. We were freezing, and there was no heating in that big dining room.

During our flight south to Yunnan, we passed over the Yangtze River, which forms China's north-south divide. I explained to Toby how the heating system works in China. The government controls heating and air conditioning in most buildings, private as well as public. The turning on and off of heating and cooling systems is arbitrarily decreed by the authorities and has nothing to do with the weather. On a bureaucratically set date in October, the heating comes on, and on a specified date in March, it is switched off. Central heating is available only north of the Yangtze. Winters can be quite cold in the south as well. We were not staying in luxurious five-star hotels but in more economical guest houses. None of the rooms had individual heaters, and we were chilled to the bone. We put it down to a China experience with which we would regale our friends later.

To keep warm, we spent a lot of time in the hotel bar, which, unlike the cavernous dining room, was smaller. The heat from our bodies and drinks kept us relatively warm. Toby was befriended by the resident dog, who happily jumped on her lap and allowed himself to be petted—until he decided he'd had enough and bit her. Since the mongrel drew blood, this set us off in search of rabies shots.

Our first stop was the local hospital. The doctor, who spoke a little English, gave us a note with an address where we could get the rabies shots. Toby was horrified that a doctor in a hospital was smoking in front of his patients. I was equally fascinated to see the long tube of ash hanging dangerously from his cigarette and waited to see if it would fall on his papers. I never did find out whether that long tubular ash ever landed on his desk, because as soon as we got his note, we rushed in a cab to the rabies hospital.

The taxi drove us out of Kunming, and as we left habitation behind, we began wondering if we had made a bad choice trusting a cabbie who spoke no English. Were we being kidnapped? After what seemed like an eternity, we saw a single building—more like a shack— in the distance. The driver pulled up in front, and two old hags came out to greet us. They reminded me of the witches in Macbeth. They beckoned us in and, with toothless smiles, produced a syringe, indicating to Toby to bare her arm. Toby was nervous, and so was I, but I tried not to show it. She held on to me for dear life as she was given the injection.

Every few days, as we continued our travels, she had to have the next shot until she had completed the course. To our relief, it all worked out in the end. We put this down, once again, to another "China experience."

Apart from the rabies scare, Yunnan exceeded our expectations. Its breathtaking beauty is something that will remain indelibly in my mind.

In Kunming, we visited the world-famous Petrified Forest. Our guide, a Naxi tribesman, spoke good English. We climbed over, under, and through the labyrinthine limestone karsts, which had been whipped and chiseled by the weather over several millennia. It was hard to believe that these formations had once been at the bottom of the sea. Our Naxi guide explained that the forest had a special meaning for his people, who were animists. I sensed it had a mystical attraction.

Toby and I traveled by bus into the Yunnan mountains and visited the cities of Dali and Lijiang. The scenery was amazing. We saw acres and acres of terraced rice fields, snow-capped mountain peaks, and oxen plowing in rice paddies. During bus stops, the local people surrounded our bus, urging us to buy their beautifully crafted pieces—blue-dyed batik cloth, embroidery, and bags. They distinguished themselves from the Han Chinese by their colorful attire—with intricate embroidery, beadwork, and headdresses. They were always smiling.

We also drove past Lake Lugu, home of the matriarchal Moso people. A few months later, during a reception at the French embassy in Beijing, I met Yang Erche Namu, who was promoting her book *Leaving Mother Lake: A Girlhood at the Edge of the World*. She describes growing up among the Moso—the last matrilineal society in the world—along Lake Lugu. Having seen it for myself, I could relate to the veneration her people have for the lake and its surroundings.

Toby and I failed to realize that we were climbing the Himalayan plateau, and once we reached Lijiang, we both were fatigued and out of breath. It was altitude sickness. We had to take it easy until we had acclimated.

Among the many other China experiences on that trip was the sharing of latrines with a group of Chinese women. The trip from Kunming to Dali was fairly long, and the bus driver stopped for a comfort break. The men got off the bus first and went into the restroom—a long, one-story, stuccoed building. I thought, "Aha, it's long, so it must have several stalls inside." When the men came out, it was our turn. The single long room was dimly lit, and there were no stalls. Instead, a long ditch stretched the length of the room with no partitions. The stench was enough to stem one's need. I froze in the doorway, but the women behind pushed past me and proceeded to answer nature's call. Once again, it was an occasion of when in Rome... The term "cheek to cheek" takes on a different meaning under these circumstances. I had heard of these toilets. Now, I had my very own first-hand experience.

***

In 2003, I lived through the SARS (Severe Acute Respiratory Syndrome) pandemic, which began in China. While the whole world was taking precautions and travelers were advised not to visit China, the local mayor assured us that there was "no SARS in Beijing." But at night, under cover of darkness, the dead were taken away in body bags. Schools were closing, and several foreign companies sent their staff home. When the outbreak spread to other countries, the government was forced to admit the presence of SARS. In true communist fashion, it sacked its minister of health and other officials, including the mayor of Beijing.

As the pandemic escalated, people rushed to stock up on rice and other comestibles, emptying shop shelves. Face masks and hand sanitizers appeared everywhere. A kind colleague, Esther, gave me a huge bag of rice to see me through. It would take me a month of Sundays to consume, but for a Chinese person, it would barely last a couple of weeks.

My friend Caroline was on an internal flight to Beijing from Sichuan. A passenger on board started coughing and feeling unwell. As soon as the plane landed, all passengers and crew were placed in quarantine. They had to stay in their apartments for ten days. Since I could not visit Caroline, I kept in touch by phone. Her company delivered cooked meals and left them outside her door. One day she called me and said: "Guess what? I have a roommate!"

"You have what?"

"I have a roommate."

"Have they foisted another quarantined person on you? I thought you weren't supposed to see anyone until they gave you the all-clear."

"Actually, he came of his own volition, and he's most welcome."

"What on earth are you talking about? If they catch you breaking your quarantine, they'll kick you out."

"Relax!" she laughed. "It's a little gecko who came in through the window, and he's my only companion. But he's rather sweet and most welcome." I took some English magazines and food and left them outside her apartment. I didn't leave any food for the gecko, as I didn't know his dietary needs.

During the pandemic, we were advised to restrict our forays into the streets. Taking advantage of the general hysteria, I ventured out and visited Beijing temples, parks, and other sites in relative freedom, without the usual jostling, shoving, and pushing of crowds. I shopped in the almost deserted shopping malls and went out with other diehard friends. Even the jackhammers seemed less noisy.

In the streets, it was not unusual to see a person remove their mask to spit or smoke. Old habits die hard, and it appeared that SARS could not extinguish them. The Chinese government tried to educate its citizens about hygiene and to discourage public spitting but with little success. When I was young and growing up in England, I remember seeing "No Spitting" and "No Smoking" signs on buses and trains, but I never saw anyone spit in public.

Many Beijing inhabitants suffered from lung infections because of the cold and pollution. Spitting had developed into a kind of art form. There seemed to be a technique involved in expectorating phlegm. First, you heard the clearing of the throat, then an intake of breath as the rising glob was gathered slowly but surely into the back of the throat, and then, in one quick whoosh, it was expertly expelled through the mouth. If you were unlucky to be in the vicinity of the projectile, you stood a good chance of becoming its recipient. One of the less pleasant aspects of walking in the streets of any Chinese city.

"Why do they do it?" I asked a friend.

"Because it's not good keeping all that phlegm inside you. You have to get rid of it."

"OK. But why spit on the ground? Can't they use a paper hankie?"

"Chinese do not use paper hankies. The doctors advise us to get rid of the phlegm."

"Even in front of others?"

"It's a matter of education. I think just before the Olympics, the authorities will ban it, as it will create a bad impression with visitors."

"Do you think people will obey?" I asked.

"They will, for a while. At least during the Games, because they will be fined, and they too want to make a good impression. Once the Games are over, they will revert to their old habits."

"I guess we are creatures of habit," I replied. "But this is one habit I'd like to see disappear."

During SARS I was helping a friend purchase a new watch. We took advantage of the quiet that prevailed and stepped into a shop. As we looked at several samples in a display cabinet, another group came in. Our view of the display was obstructed by bodies. I should have realized that if you leave so much as an inch of space in front of you, someone will fill it. The concept of keeping your distance or having your own space is non-existent in a city of 24 million. I took off my mask and began to cough—louder and louder. I kept it up for a few minutes and made a big show of it. Soon, the entire shop emptied. We quickly concluded our business, but not before we got a good price from the nervous assistant.

Sixteen years later, the same virus, now metamorphosed as Covid-19, sent the world into panic. Hundreds of thousands died. This time I took it seriously and kept away from crowds, following all the necessary precautions. I had been lucky in China. When I came to the USA in 2006, the lackadaisical attitude of Washington—their negligence and lies about the Covid outbreak in 2020 were similar to the tactics employed by the Chinese authorities back in 2003.

***

As part of its preparations for the Games, the Chinese authorities sent questionnaires requesting suggestions from foreign companies and schools. They wanted to make the capital more welcoming to visitors. The city had an inordinate number of signs in Chinglish. They were everywhere—indoors, outdoors, and in most public places. The authorities realized they had to brush up on their English. Xinhua news agency promised that Beijing city authorities would issue new translation guides. In the meantime, the signs provided a great deal of amusement for us: "Don't Bother" instead of "Do Not Disturb," a dog park in Beijing labeled, "Dog Bark," a paragliding site described as "Site of jumping umbrella." The Beijing Bureau of Tourism set up a hotline for visitors and residents to report examples of bad English. I tried to contact them a couple of times, but not surprisingly, the line was always busy.

In Hong Kong, our maids were called "amahs" but in Beijing they are called "ayi," which means aunt. In the PRC (People's Republic of China), we hired our aunties to clean our homes, babysit our kids, and empty the trash. My ayi, who had a good head for heights, even washed my "nonexistent" fourth-floor windows. She was a great help since she was willing to stand in line and pay my gas, telephone, and electricity bills. I looked forward to her coming once a week, and after each visit, my flat sparkled. If she thought I looked under the weather, she cooked for me.

The north of China grows wheat and not as much rice as the south. Our Beijing diet consisted largely of noodles and dumplings. Steaming Mongolian hotpots kept us warm in winter. To this day, I enjoy having friends round for a Steam Boat meal, where the cooking is done at the table.

When eating out, I learned not to trust the mangled English translations on the menus. How could I bring myself to order: "Paleolithic mushrooms," "Fried prig," or "Digestible Squib"? If I didn't have someone who spoke Chinese with me, I walked among the tables and saw what the other guests were eating. If a dish caught my eye, I'd point to it, and the waiter added it to my order. Sometimes, a young eager-beaver student asked if he or she could help, often with mixed results.

Eating out is part of the culture and way of life in China, a custom I thoroughly enjoyed. Most Chinese people are very loyal to their region's cuisine, and they tend to deride the dishes of other areas. One Beijing friend told me: "The Cantonese will eat anything that moves," and my friends from Hong Kong made equally disparaging comments about northern food. Their dislike of each other's cuisine was mutual.

Whenever Chinese people want to engage a foreigner in conversation, one of the most frequently used openings is: "Do you like Chinese food?" Many times when I answered "yes," they would drag me to a nearby Chinese eatery for more English conversation. After a while, I employed a ruse by stating "I don't understand," and this left me some room to wriggle out of any further questions. I did not want to hurt their feelings, but I could not allow myself to be constantly diverted down side lanes when I was short on time.

My friend, Tommy Wu, a native of Sichuan, which is famous for its hot spicy food, always took me to a Sichuan restaurant. Once there, he would extol the medicinal benefits of each dish and its ingredients. He sounded like a medical encyclopedia. From my time in Hong Kong, I knew that Chinese hosts are prone to do this. I also noticed that when ordering, Tommy engaged the waiter in deep discussion about the way each dish was prepared, its freshness, and any additions or changes desired. Very much a case of al gusto—as you wish. The one time I took Tommy to a Cantonese eatery, he refused to order and made a big show of it. He banged the menu on the table saying, "I can't order any of this. I don't know the food!"

Tommy was a real character. During WWII, when China was on our side and busy fighting the Japanese invaders, he was sent to the USA to train as a pilot. World War II ended before he completed his training, and he was summoned back to China. When the Communists came to power in 1949, he was regarded with great suspicion. For years they interrogated him, incarcerated him, tortured him, and exiled him.

Years later, in 1989, Tommy was commissioned to sculpt a bronze bust of the American journalist Edgar Snow. He returned to the US in 1989 where he lectured on art and sculpture at the University of Missouri in Kansas City. His autobiography, *The Sparrow's Voice— Living Through China's Turmoil in the 20th Century,* is not so much the story of China but a story about the amazing strength and resilience of the human spirit. He showed no bitterness for the many years stolen from him.

By the time I met him, Tommy was in his eighties and often acted as my guide around the capital. When my friend Toby came to Beijing, the three of us went out for a meal. Tommy reminisced about his time in America. Then, to the delight and surprise of staff and patrons, Toby and Tommy started singing: "Kiss Me Goodnight Sergeant Major," "Praise the Lord and Pass the Ammunition," "I'll Be Seeing You," "Off We Go Into The Wild Blue Yonder," and "Boogie Woogie Bugle Boy," all World War II-era songs.

While in the US, Tommy learned English by listening to the radio and memorized the songs of that period. Toby and Tommy made a good team. I offered, tongue-in-cheek, to be their manager on their next concert tour.

Unfortunately, Tommy is no longer with us, but his memory lingers on for those who knew him. He was a kind, gentle man, and I felt sad that he had suffered so much at the hands of his countrymen.

***

Before I left London, a couple I knew from church gave me their son's contact details in China. They asked me to look him up if I ever were in his neck of the woods. During a school break, Caroline and I visited his city on the east coast. He took us to a Brazilian steakhouse. It was quite an experience—the meats kept coming in all shapes and forms, but only in one size: ginormous. I had never seen steaks and chunks of meat that big before. Even more memorable was the conversation I had with our host. After the usual introductions, I asked him what brought him to China.

"I am the Durex condom representative," he replied.

"For this region?"

"No, for the whole of China."

"Then business must be brisk and profitable with the one-child policy," I said.

"It's not."

"Why? I thought the government wants to restrict the birth rate. Surely this must be good for your business?"

"In China, birth control is considered to be the woman's responsibility. The men don't bother to take precautions."

"But aren't they worried about unwanted pregnancies?"

"If the woman gets pregnant, she is forced to have an abortion... We tried to educate the males, we even offered free prophylactics in their workplace, and in their neighborhoods, but with little success."

This surprised me. "One of the few positive measures taken by the communist party is the emancipation of women, affording them equal rights, and abolishing concubinage," I said.

"Well, this is one area where they haven't made much progress," he replied. "Single women are fitted with the coil, the internal contraceptive. These are crudely made and they cause the women many problems and health issues."

"Then why do they use them?"

"They have no choice. And, they have annual checks to ensure that they are still in place and working. It's obligatory."

When we returned to Beijing, I asked my Chinese girlfriends about this, and they all confirmed his story. They had all been fitted with the internal contraceptive coil, whether they wanted it or not. Even married couples had to wait for the government's go-ahead for that one baby. Birth control for married couples worked on a rotation system, and each prospective mother had to wait for "approval" to get pregnant. A couple of decades later they were to rue the results of the single-child policy.

The one-child policy did not apply to ethnic minorities. Also exempted were parents who had master's degrees. If both mother and father had a master's degree, they were allowed to have two children based on the general belief that they had to be clever to have a master's degree, and if both parents with master's degrees had children, their children would have high IQs. I wondered whether eugenics was behind this decision.

To a Westerner, this was perhaps incomprehensible, but the Chinese population accepted the policy as a way of life—perhaps as the price they had to pay for their new prosperity. With both parents working, delaying having a family might be welcomed. Once the child was born to city parents, the infant was dispatched to grandparents, sometimes 3,000 miles away. An entire generation of children was raised by grandparents.

During long school vacations, I returned to England or traveled overseas to visit my family in Australia, as well as my son Iain and his family in New Zealand. Abroad, people often asked me: "Do you feel safe?" or "How safe is it living in a Communist country?" and even, "Do they spy on you? Have they bugged your place?" I felt duty-bound to assure them that I felt safer in China than walking the streets of London. And as for being spied upon, since I had nothing to hide, I had nothing to fear. Should the government decide that I was not welcome, they could revoke my visa and ask me to leave.

Of course, I was careful not to discuss politics or religion with strangers. I knew that certain subjects were never to be mentioned, either in telephone or email conversations. When an Australian colleague told me that her husband's email and internet service vanished for four months, I asked why.

"Someone sent him an email asking about the Tiananmen Square incident and the democracy movement."

"And..?"

"His emails all disappeared and he could not use the internet."

That struck me as rather drastic, but... When in Rome... I had not gone to China to change its political system or to become an activist. What we consider activism in the West is considered troublemaking in China. Since my reasons for going there were purely financial, I had to accept the fact that the vast majority of its population was satisfied with the way their country was being run.

I did, however, have one memorable experience when I thought I might get into trouble, and perhaps even arrested. I was with an overseas visitor in Beijing's Tiananmen Square, where a huge portrait of Chairman Mao stared down at us. It was a cold winter day, and we wanted to use the bathroom. Public conveniences are scarce in that area. We located one and headed there.

Outside stood a two-legged, female toilet paper dispenser. She was a portly, no-nonsense Party worker, dispensing toilet paper to those who wanted to use the facility. She issued me one 5 by 5-inch square. I politely asked for some more, and she brusquely told me that was all I would get! I was being rationed!

With icy winds blowing down from the Mongolian steppes, I was not going to argue with this human machine. Our need was becoming more urgent by the minute. Without a second thought, I grabbed the roll from her, helped myself to what I felt was my due ration, and did the same for my friend.

The toilet dispenser was furious, cursing us in Chinese. She motioned to a couple of guards nearby, who simply looked away and walked off, apparently reluctant to get involved. Who wants to mediate between a toilet paper dispenser and a foreigner? Besides, this foreigner could be someone important—a diplomatic incident might ensue. If the Western press got hold of it, they would not pass up the opportunity to write disparaging comments about paper rationing in the country that had invented paper. It was a well-known fact that in China, when you left your hotel, you carried toilet paper with you. Can you imagine the headlines? "Tourist arrested over toilet paper issue," or "Western bums require more toilet paper."

When I told Tommy about what happened, he suggested that the worker may have rationed the paper so that she could take the remainder of the roll home. She probably did a roaring trade on the black market in "recycled" bathroom tissue.

**

Under socialism, people are urged to work hard for a better tomorrow. They are placed in collectives and given targets to accomplish in one to five-year plans. In China, it was obvious that hard work had paid off. The Chinese enjoyed freedom and comforts they never had before. No longer were they forced into collectives. They could buy and sell their houses, spend money on luxuries, buy cars, cell phones, and computers, as well as travel abroad. Palatial shopping malls—cathedrals of opulence—offered haute couture with brand names such as Yves St. Laurent, Dior, Gucci, Cartier, and Waterford. Everything that Fifth Avenue or Rodeo Drive could offer. There were of course the fakes— fake Cartier watches, fake designer clothes and accessories—all at knock-down prices. But at least there was a choice.

All this prosperity and luxury was akin to the soma of Aldous Huxley's *Brave New World*—lulling the people into soporific passivity. Amazed and dazzled by their country's transformation, they were on a roll, little caring that their prosperity was the byproduct of a totalitarian regime. As Deng Xiaoping said: "What does it matter if it's a black cat or a white cat? As long as it catches mice, it's a good cat."

***

In 2005, my younger son Alistair was getting married in London. The previous year I had paid off my mortgage. I had achieved the main purpose of going to the Far East. I decided to return to England for the wedding and repair my home—badly damaged by a squatter tenant. I was not sure whether I would return to the Middle Kingdom, but I kept a few doors open.

I might have gone to China with a few preconceived ideas, even prejudices. Thankfully, many were overturned when I immersed myself in the country's culture. As Mark Twain said: "Travel is fatal to prejudice, bigotry, and narrow-mindedness..." Valid today, as in 1919. I left with a myriad of beautiful and unusual memories, including an Easter Sunrise service on the Great Wall of China. Our church, at the 21st Century Hotel, organized the trip. One Easter Sunday, before dawn, we boarded several buses and headed for the Great Wall. We were the only group there, huddled together under the stars, singing hymns and celebrating one of Christendom's greatest festivals. It felt surreal. Suddenly, the sun burst through illuminating us—a bunch of Christian laowai singing and praising the resurrection of Jesus on the Great Wall of China. Did I feel safe in China? Yes, sir! I did.

I was leaving behind many friends and a comfortable lifestyle. I had survived the SARS epidemic and accomplished my main objectives– –to become debt-free and to get to know another country. I felt glad to have witnessed a great nation's transformation and amazing changes— some good and some worrisome, but the fact that I had lived to see them was itself a great privilege.

Now, it was time for change in my own life—time to turn the page and start a new chapter. Also, I had started internet dating.

CHAPTER SEVEN

HOME AGAIN

I returned to England in 2005. From previous experience, I knew that settling back into life in the UK would take time. However, I was pleasantly surprised to get a couple of jobs fairly quickly. The local Council hired me to teach English to refugees who had applied for UK citizenship. They were an interesting group, mostly from the Middle East and Afghanistan. It is nigh impossible to teach a group of Middle Easterners without mentioning food, and sooner or later, I was invited to their homes for a meal. The first invitation came from Sara, an Iraqi student. As soon as we entered her apartment, she removed her headscarf and hijab. I couldn't take my eyes off her beautiful brown hair and her Dior pantsuit. "Sara, you're beautiful. Don't you feel uncomfortable wearing the scarf and hijab all the time when you're outside?"

"No, we're used to it. It's much hotter in my country, and it's our custom."

"But how about Anita? She doesn't wear the hijab, and she's a Muslim."

"She's from Albania. I don't know; you have to ask her."

During my visit, her husband walked in with a male friend. Sara immediately disappeared into the bedroom to return covered. What a palaver, I thought.

My other job was working again as an IELTS (International English Language Testing System) examiner for Cambridge University. I had to test foreign professionals—doctors, pharmacists, engineers, architects—and decide whether their English was adequate for them to work in England in their professions. I was busy working two jobs, getting my house repaired, and looking forward to Alistair and Kathrin's wedding.

Kathrin's Swiss family arrived for the wedding in a minibus. I was to meet them at the pre-nuptial dinner the day before the wedding. During the meal, I presented Kathrin with a pearl necklace from China. Her father looked at it and asked in German: "Sind sie echt?" to which I replied, also in German: "Of course, what do you think—that I would give her fake ones?" Poor chap, he had not been warned that the future mother-in-law spoke German.

As always, London offers a variety of interesting things to do and see—art galleries, museums, theatres, concerts, and movies. The city had just been chosen to host the 2012 Olympics. I penned an article describing Beijing's preparations for its own Olympics, still three years away. It was accepted for publication, but on the same day—7 July 2005—London was violently attacked by Muslim extremists. I was able to amend my article to include the bomb attacks, and it was published in the evening edition.

The World Wide Web was becoming increasingly pervasive in all aspects of life. I had started internet dating while I lived in China, and after a few mismatches, I was unimpressed. I then asked David, a friend, what he thought of it. "I don't know much about it," he said, "but I heard that eHarmony has good results."

On his recommendation, I signed up with eHarmony, which differs from other dating sites because its connections are based on algorithms. Had it not been for David's recommendation, I would have given up once I saw the application process. The first step was to fill out a long questionnaire of some 450 questions. It took me a couple of weeks to complete. The questions were thorough—about my beliefs, values, emotional health, skills, education, character, and appearance. There were also specific questions as to what I was looking for and who I considered to be my "ideal" match. It reminded me of the psychometric tests job applicants endure. One question dealt with the geographical "catchment" area of my search. How far did I want to spread my net? On previous sites, I had restricted myself to the United Kingdom, but as I had lived and traveled in so many countries, I went for the worldwide option. Mine was indeed a www search! And why not?

Finally, I completed the questionnaire and paid my dues. Now, it was up to the computer to find me a suitable match. Unlike previous dating sites, I never got to see or choose a possible suitor. Only after the gremlins inside the computer found someone with a profile matching mine was, I told, "We have a match for you." The first two prospects were no matches at all. They could hardly write or spell. The only way they communicated was with forwards. I wanted to know what they were thinking and what they had done—not other people's funny jokes or quotes.

After a couple of mismatches, "John from Rio Rancho" popped up. I took one look at his picture and thought, Hmm... he looks like an aged hippy who ended up in some banana republic in South America. I couldn't even find a country called Rio Rancho. Since eHarmony recommends that the female make the first contact, I sent "John from Rio Rancho" a one-sentence introduction, thinking I would never hear back. I wasn't particularly interested, and South America was not on my bucket list.

Surprisingly, he responded immediately, and so began a correspondence that resulted, five months later, in our marriage in the beautiful New Mexico mountain village of Jemez Springs.

During our five-month correspondence/courtship, John put me right: New Mexico was not in South America but part of the United States of America. Rio Rancho was not a country but a city and a suburb of Albuquerque. My education about all things American had begun—and it continues to this day.

Soon after that first exchange of emails, John came to London to meet me. He must have liked what he saw, and one morning, he got down on one knee and proposed. Most of my previous "suitors" wanted to bed me; John wanted to wed me. "Will you marry me?" he asked.

"But you don't know me," I blurted.

"I know enough," he replied.

That was more than a decade ago. We soon discovered we had a great deal in common. We agreed on most fundamentals: religion, politics, morals, and education. Both book lovers, we had read the works of the same poets and novelists. He had worked as an editor on several provincial newspapers and I had my BBC background. He had also lived in Germany and was familiar with England and Europe. He was recently widowed after 48 years of marriage, and his children, like mine, were grown up, married, and independent. His late wife was also from England.

Not long after we began to correspond, John told me that his friends and family called him JD—the initials for John Davidson. Americans tend to use initials in lieu of a full name, something we don't do in England. They also use nicknames. "Please call me JD," he said, "because every time you write 'Dear John,' I think of it as a 'dear John letter.'"

My family and friends had misgivings. They disliked the idea of internet dating. It was not common at the time, and people "our age" did not look for mates on the internet. Personal columns in local newspaper classified sections served as dating opportunities. Some friends also questioned my decision to go to America.

My cousin Don kept saying, "But America! Why America?" Don believes that civilization began in Greece and ended in Western Europe. He could not comprehend that China, India, Egypt, and the Americas had their own cultures and civilizations. Of course, this was ignorance on his part. He is wholly embedded and wedded to the idea that Greece is exceptional and the fount of all wisdom and beauty. Little did I suspect that I would encounter the same mindset in my new country.

In England, few knew where New Mexico was. When John tried to explain that it was between Texas and Arizona, most Brits had no idea where those states were either. Don kept saying, "Why don't you go to the civilized parts, like New York or San Francisco?" He too, had no idea where New Mexico was—and if he didn't know, it wasn't worth knowing. At least, that was his take on things.

Everyone rushed to give me advice and to spell out their prejudices about the United States. My friend Ruth, who had visited the States, warned: "The only people you'll have anything in common with will be the Americans who have traveled and lived abroad." She even did an internet search on John to make sure I wasn't marrying a Bluebeard.

My younger son Alistair, who had lived in Texas for six months, also came up with advice: "Mum, Americans are very patriotic. They don't like criticism and will not admit that there's anything wrong with their country." Then he added, "Their mustard is terrible, and so is their cheese. What they call 'Swiss' cheese is edible rubber." He is married to a Swiss girl and could tell the difference. Ruth also advised, "Whenever you use an American recipe, just halve the sugar." This last piece of information was the most useful.

Even my American friend Paula, for whom the "Wild West" begins half a mile west of Manhattan, advised caution: "You should go out there and see for yourself," she said. "Go and check it out, and see what it's like before you commit."

John's family was equally cautious about this new woman from across the Pond, who was about to become their new step-mum, step-granny, step everything.

Before he came to London, John's sister admonished him: "Now don't go and do something silly and come back married!"

He did not return married but engaged—soon-to-be-married.

After we announced our engagement, John returned to New Mexico, and I went into panic mode. I had only a couple of months to sort out my life and my things, find tenants for my London home (again), and say goodbye to friends and family. Was I excited? Yes. Was I panicking? Yes. Was I scared? Yes. Did I have second thoughts? Yes. But I went ahead with my preparations. If I can survive China, I can survive the USA.

Our wedding details were arranged with his family by email, telephone, and Skype. His two daughters were gracious and accepted me—or rather, they accepted and respected their father's decision. Their mother had passed away less than a year ago, and here was the patriarch bringing a new wife into their lives.

Patriarch is a good way to describe John. His four children are strong believers in reproducing their genes and gave him 18 grandchildren—his eldest daughter had eight children. As an only child, I felt that I had done my duty to humankind by birthing twice. His younger daughter, Maellen, sent me the family tree. It took me a while to remember all the names of his tribe, who was who, and who belonged to whom, but it helped.

The only family member opposed to our marriage was John's eldest son, Ben. He had joined a religious cult that bans divorced people from remarrying. This cult bans a lot of things, including the use of cars, electricity, radios, cameras, and tolerance. He warned his father that he would go to hell if he went ahead with the wedding. He was the only fly in the ointment—but thankfully, this particular fly lived in a different state. Subsequently, I discovered that for years, he had shunned every member of his extended family, convinced that only his brand of religiosity would get him into heaven. I guess every family has a black sheep.

On 28 June 2006, forewarned and with two huge suitcases, I arrived at Albuquerque's Sunport Airport to be met by my future husband. During our many emails and phone calls, I asked John not to come with his entire clan. I had nightmares of a grand tribal reception with placards and balloons declaring: "WELCOME TO THE USA NORA." To my mind, it was the American way of doing things—but not the British way.

John arrived with only one granddaughter, Heather, to help with my luggage. He came in some sort of rusty, musty-smelling contraption, which I later learned is called a "truck." I was wearing a long, tight skirt and high heels, and there was no running board on the truck. I inelegantly hitched up my skirt—as far up as modesty allowed—and climbed into the vehicle while Heather and John lugged my bags to the back.

On the way home, John pointed out the various sights and landmarks. To the left: "This is Albuquerque." I looked, and all I could see were a couple of tall buildings. "Where?"

"There!" and he gestured toward the two buildings. Two tall buildings! Is that what Albuquerque is all about... the biggest city in New Mexico? Then, as we drove over a bridge, he pointed to the wadi below: "This is the Rio Grande," he said.

This dry wadi is the famous Rio Grande? Where was the Rio Grande of the movies—the frontier with Mexico where the hero and banditos had to cross waist-high in water? Was this the same Rio Grande? Later, I learned that the local word for a wadi is "arroyo."

The long flight, the excitement, and the preparations to get to NM, coupled with jet lag and altitude, left me exhausted. I was so thankful that John, my two stepdaughters, Lydia and Maellen, and my daughter-in-law, Martha, had arranged most of our wedding details. As if that wasn't enough, they had cooked and prepared meals which they placed in our freezer and refrigerator. I did not have to cook for the first couple of weeks after my arrival. I was deeply moved by their warmth and hospitality. I had heard of American generosity and kindness—now I was experiencing it firsthand.

My two sons could not attend the wedding. Iain lives in New Zealand, and the cost of the flight for three was exorbitant. Alistair was in the middle of his studies at Oxford University. Since my immediate family could not attend, I was grateful that four dear friends accepted my invitation to be there for me.

I first asked my friend Toby from San Francisco. She and I had shared many adventures in China. Toby was my Matron of Honour.

My second guest was Paula, who lives in New York City. We had met years earlier in London and had become close friends. It is a sign of our friendship that she was willing to leave Manhattan to attend our nuptials in New Mexico.

My third guest was my cousin Koulis from Maine. Koulis had served 29 years in the US Navy on nuclear submarines. In his home in Maine, he keeps a diving suit similar to the spacesuits worn by astronauts. He said he would dress in his navy uniform for the occasion. He's not going to wear that spacesuit, is he? How's he going to walk me up the aisle in that thing? I had visions of him ambling up the aisle with me by his side, trying to speed him along. As a wedding present, he sent us 10 live Maine lobsters packed in dry ice, which the driver left on the doorstep without ringing the doorbell. The ice around them was melting rapidly in the July heat. If John had not noticed them on his way to the mailbox, all ten crustaceans would have perished. We rescued them just in time. And, of course, Koulis did not wear his diver's suit at the wedding.

My fourth guest was David Aikman, who had suggested I try eHarmony. Our acquaintance went back several decades to when he was fresh out of college in England. Years later, we met again in Hong Kong when he was a Time magazine correspondent. He and his wife, Nonie, were among the friends we knew and socialized with on the island. Nonie gave us some beautiful capiz shell place mats from her native Philippines. I still use them for special occasions and value them greatly.

Two decades later, I met David again in Beijing. By this time, he had built quite a reputation as a journalist, writer, and lecturer at Patrick Henry College. He has interviewed many famous people and authored several books, including a biography of George W. Bush. John's son and daughter-in-law put him up during his stay for our wedding in New Mexico, and to their delight, David entertained them with stories about his flights on Air Force One with President Bush, and his interviews with other well-known persons. During our wedding, David read the scripture passages John and I had chosen—his clear English diction made those verses even more meaningful and brought tears to our eyes.

David and cousin Koulis walked me up the aisle—yes, I had two escorts—while 16-year-old grandson Silas, at John's request, played the Radames March from Aida on his trumpet. He played it beautifully. The church was full because John had invited everyone in Jemez Springs to our wedding. He felt he could not leave anyone out as they would be hurt. He and his late wife had lived there for 10 years, and the villagers turned up to see the new wife.

I had one surprise for John. At the end of the ceremony, his daughters, Maellen and Lydia, came forward to present me with the Davidson tartan. My friend, Betty Cosgrove, also a Davidson, had given me the Davidson sash as a wedding present. I wanted to show that I was not only marrying John but joining his clan as well.

We honeymooned in Santa Fe, and during our road trip, I saw the most beautiful desert sunsets, reflected on the red rocks of Ghost Ranch, and learned about Georgia O'Keeffe and her cohort of artists. On our return, we visited the picturesque old mining town of Madrid. I marveled at the preponderance of the color brown. It was another world, and I realized how much I had to adapt and learn.

Churchill's saying: "England and America are two countries divided by a common language," was proving to be true. The first time John said he was blowing smoke up my pant leg, my reaction was, "But you told me you don't smoke!" At the dinner table, I told him to: "Tuck in!" whereupon he stood up and tucked in his shirt. "What are you doing?" I said.

"You told me to tuck in."

"Tuck in! Means let's eat!"

I was learning a new language. "Pants" are not underwear, "sidewalk" is pavement, "hood" is a car's bonnet, and "trunk" is its boot. My friend Sandy had been driving her Jaguar car for several months with a warning light indicating: "Boot Open." She asked me what it meant. I explained that her trunk was not properly shut. I also learned that a cigarette should never be called a "fag" and that "jugs" is American slang for breasts, so I learned to call a jug a "pitcher." Americans put "gas," not petrol, in their cars, and car parks are called parking lots. It was a steep learning curve.

New Mexico, known as the Land of Enchantment, is the only American state that is officially bilingual, with documents and instructions printed in both English and Spanish. I had learned Castilian Spanish in England, but Latin American Spanish is different. It wasn't just American English that gave me problems, but also the proliferation of Spanish words in the local English. In Spain, a tortilla is an omelet; in America, it is a flatbread, similar to a Greek pitta, on which you place cooked food and then roll it up—the ubiquitous Mexican wrap. Words like acequia, mesa, luminarias, farolitos, vigas, arroyo, burritos, and adobe—just to mention a few—expanded my vocabulary. In China, I had to contend with Chinglish, and here with Spanglish!

My knowledge of US geography was also sadly lacking. I had no idea where Iowa or Kentucky were, and as for state capitals, I scored an "F." I had never heard the term "Rust Belt." I always thought that the Midwest was somewhere out there where they grew a lot of corn and cattle grazed on thousand-acre farms. When a friend of the family told me she came from Odesa, I immediately asked her: "Do you speak Russian or Ukrainian?" She looked puzzled. "No. Why would you think that?" she said.

"Because you were born in Odesa. How old were you when you came to the United States?"

"I was born in the US. I was born in Odesa, Texas."

Oops! "Oh, I'm sorry. The only Odesa I know is the one by the Black Sea. Gosh, they don't have the Black Sea here too, do they?"

I don't think she understood my joke. But from then on, whenever people ask me: "Where are you from?" I reply: "From London, England."

When I forget to add the world "England" I often get asked: "You mean London, England?"

"Yes, is there any other?" The quizzical look told me they didn't get the irony. The doubling of English place names confused me at first. When I began to correspond with John, he said that he had lived in towns named Ipswich, Gloucester, Chelmsford, Uxbridge, etc. I assumed that he knew these English towns well. Wow, he's lived and worked in England for quite some time. Until it dawned on me that these were American towns. No wonder in the States, people automatically name the city followed by the state, such as Ipswich, Mass., or Portland, Oregon.

In Europe, if you travel three to four hundred miles, you are in a different country with a different language, culture, and even religion. In the United States, there are 48 contiguous states with the same language (almost), each proud of its uniqueness. John bought me a jigsaw puzzle with all the states and their capitals, and I had great fun putting it together and trying to memorize the locations. I am still trying to remember, not very successfully, all fifty state capitals.

***

When I arrived in New Mexico on 28 June 2006, everyone was getting ready to celebrate 4 July, and many said: "Oh, you've come in time for the Fourth!" I came in time for my wedding. What's the Fourth of July? As if reading my mind, John explained that it was the anniversary of the country's Declaration of Independence in 1776. Am I supposed to celebrate this? A holiday Americans faithfully observe each year.

"We must go to Jemez Springs for the celebrations," he said. "It's a typical small-town parade, and everybody takes part." I looked forward to seeing the village and experiencing my first American public holiday. It seemed a good idea to see the place and church where we were to be married in a couple of weeks' time.

The drive to Jemez took about an hour, and on the way, John pointed out the various landmarks—the Ponderosa winery, the Feed Store in San Ysidro, and the Jemez Pueblo, which is Indian land inhabited by Native Americans. Up until then I didn't know that the first vine grapes were brought to New Mexico by the Spanish. I thought a feed store was a quaint name for a roadside inn and that "pueblo" was simply the Spanish word for a hamlet or village. How far was everything from London, Greece, Beijing, or Hong Kong! It was exciting and new, but I was also apprehensive, wondering where I would fit into this strange new environment.

We arrived early because the only road into the village of Jemez Springs—also its Main Street—was closed during the parade. We sat under an apricot tree on the grounds of the Presbyterian church facing the road. I sensed the excitement as people started lining the street with their dogs, kids, strollers, and folding chairs.

Just as the excitement reached its climax, a cacophony of music assaulted our ears. A group of young people marched past, their instruments making a merry sound and looking very pleased with their efforts. From the loud cheering and clapping, I guessed that the proud parents were standing on the sidelines. Then came an array of floats representing the local school, credit union, library, and music camp down the road. But the loudest applause was reserved for the fire trucks and the firemen. As they drove by, they threw candy at the children and bystanders. John explained that the woods and forests around the Jemez mountains are prone to fires. The labs in nearby Los Alamos were threatened by fires on several occasions. Firemen in the Jemez Valley are kept busy throughout the long, dry summer season. No wonder they are so highly thought of and appreciated.

And then it was over. I blinked—and it was over. Like Oliver Twist, I wanted more, but the parade, the marchers, floats, and bands had been and gone. There was a genuine joie de vivre in the proceedings, and bystanders looked happy. Though simple and small by comparison to big city parades, the entire village had put its heart and soul into the celebration. The warmth, pride, and love were almost tangible.

Since then, I have been to several parades for various holidays and celebrations. Americans love putting on a good show and corral everyone to join in. The disabled veterans parade in their wheelchairs; there are bands—some good, some bad, and some indifferent—floats, horseback riders, motorcycles, cheerleaders, cars, marchers, kids, seniors, prom queens—all making a joyful sound, and cheerfully waving to those standing on the sidelines. Everyone takes part. I have often described it as an orchestrated cacophony of sounds. I have to admit that I too, enjoy the shows and celebrate with the best of them—even 4 July!

As soon as the parade was over, John suggested we have lunch at "Los Ojos."

"Where's that?"

"Right next door. Let's go."

Here was another first for me. It was, I was told, a typical southwestern bar. The walls were covered with stuffed animals—some in their entirety and some just the head—animal skins, horns, guns, and other hunting trophies. To me, it exuded a "cowboy ambiance." No need to go to the zoo. Just look at the stuffed bobcats, bears, and elks.

It was time I had my first T-bone steak. John is not a steak person; more of a ground beef man. It arrived sizzling hot, done to perfection, with vegetables and mashed potatoes. It's different from the Mandarin Hotel in Hong Kong and the Ritz in London, but the people here are a lot friendlier and more interesting! When is the bar brawl going to start, and when is John Wayne going to burst through those doors? Flashbacks from Westerns raced through my mind.

After we were married, we often drove up to Jemez Springs to attend Sunday service, followed by lunch at Los Ojos. Most of the congregation disembarked there after church. The smell of pine trees, the rustling of the wind, and the rich autumn colors of the aspens and cottonwoods brought back childhood memories. They reminded me of the Troodos mountains of my native island of Cyprus.

Several residents of Santa Fe and Albuquerque own second homes in the Jemez and enjoy the cooler breezes, hiking trails, and village life. But the heart of the village is the people who have made it their permanent home—artists, writers, scientists, and retirees. For me, it was the ideal escape from Albuquerque's dry heat.

I soon realized that John had a sweet tooth. He needed his daily fix of chocolate in any shape or size. I had some inkling of this when we first met in London. A couple of days after his arrival, he started looking drawn and uncomfortable. "Do you have any candy?" he asked. "What?" "Umm... I think you call it chocolate here in the UK." "Oh, I see. No... I don't have any. I don't have young children, so why would I keep chocolate in the house?" I realized he needed candy, so I bought him some—whereupon he relaxed and looked much happier. My doubts about his addiction were confirmed soon after we married. Each time we passed a Dunkin' Donuts franchise, he'd point it out and say, "Ah, look! Doughnuts!" He would turn and gaze longingly in the direction of the shop. "Please keep your eyes on the road and mind the traffic." Each time he got distracted, I got nervous. "Shall we go in and have a doughnut?" "I'm not very hungry." "You don't have to be hungry to have a doughnut." "Let's do take-out." So we'd stop briefly, and he'd go into the shop for his doughnut. A doughnut was the understatement of the century. I quickly found out that Americans don't buy just *a* doughnut. They feel obligated to buy a box of at least six, or even twelve, which they happily share. Spread the happiness—and the diabetes—with it, babe.

John told me that breakfast was his favorite meal, whereas I have never been a breakfast person. My idea of breakfast is a cup of tea with a piece of toast or some cold cereal wolfed down on the hoof. Many times, I go without and never miss it. He kept mentioning his favorite place: "I have to take you to Weck's. We should have brunch there soon. They have the best breakfast in town." I couldn't refuse this sugar-breakfast-donuts-cookies-candy addict. So, one Saturday morning, we went to the nearest Weck's. As soon as we sat down, a server poured us a glass of water. Well... actually, most of it was ice.

I looked around, and my first thought was: *this must be an obese person's convention.* Most of the patrons seemed too big for their chairs, with parts of their lower anatomy hanging over the sides. They were eating with great gusto, demolishing huge portions. Some customers even had big slabs of meat on their plates. In no time, we were presented with menus and more coffee. I took one look at the menu, and my eyes glazed over—my mind went into meltdown. There was so much choice. I thought our English breakfast covered all the bases, but this was indeed *embarras de richesses*—a confusing abundance.

There were more than half a dozen types of omelets with exotic names, such as The Olde Time Favourite, The Abney, The Big Pig, and The South of Denver Omelette. There was even a Build Your Own Omelette option, starting with four eggs. They contained equally exotic ingredients—guacamole, chili, and jack cheeses. Below the omelets was a list of pancakes: full-stack, short-stack, and even a pancake sandwich. Then came variations of French toast, followed by waffles, and finally, the most exotic item of all: burritos. I was definitely out of my depth with items such as *carne adovada* and *pollo*. I couldn't make up my mind. I needed a dictionary. What happened to the humble bacon, eggs, and one sausage? Finally, I decided to go for the Build Your Own Omelette. We were ready to order. The server came to our table with a pen and notebook in hand.

"Wha'd ya like in it, honey?"

"Just an omelette, no honey. Thank you," I replied. She gave me a funny look.

"Ya wanna both cheddar and jack cheese?" Not wanting to appear ignorant, I said, "Yes, please," hoping that would be the end of it.

But she continued: "Bell peppers and mushrooms?"

"No, thank you." Thinking: *Please go! Just take my order and go.*

"Diced tomatoes, spinach, sprouts?"

"No, thanks."

"Sour cream?" "No, thanks."

"With grits?" I had no idea what grits were, but I knew I didn't want them. "No, thanks!"

"With hash browns, mashed potatoes or chips?"

This time, with gritted teeth: "No, thanks." Just go!

"Biscuits and gravy?"

"No, thanks."

"Red or green?"

"Excuse me?"

"Red or green?"

What on earth had traffic lights got to do with a simple omelet? "Red" or "Green". Did she mean stop or go? I had no idea.

This was ridiculous and very confusing. There seemed no end to the choices. My husband watched all this with a wry smile. Finally, he came to my rescue and explained that red or green meant chili.

"You put chili in your omelets?"

"Yeah! This is the Southwest. We put chili on everything."

At last, the waitress left with our order. In the meantime, I seemed unable to finish my coffee. A server kept appearing from nowhere, topping up my cup when I wasn't looking. I was too busy watching the clientele and marveling at the copious amounts of food they devoured. After a short wait, our breakfast arrived. A stack of pancakes for John with his Spanish omelet and my order. The pancakes were frisbee-sized, and the omelets gargantuan. They too, spilled over the edge of our plates—just like the derrières of the patrons. I lost my appetite. John, who is skinny as a rake, couldn't finish his Lucullan meal either. We ended up taking most of it home in the proverbial doggy bag. I had to summon the courage to tell my husband that I never wanted to go to Weck's again—without hurting his feelings. I realize that diners are embedded in the American psyche with their comfort food and fast service, but they were not my cup of tea. I found the solution: each year, on Father's Day or any other festive occasion, his kids take him to Weck's for breakfast.

***

It was not long before we realized that we needed a bigger house. John's handweaving and part-time writing required space. His looms occupied an entire room, and I was expecting 76 boxes to arrive from the UK with my personal belongings. John said we needed to get a realtor––another new word for me. In England, estate agents find prospective buyers and show them available homes. The paperwork is done by an attorney or a paralegal.

John organized the sale of the house and hired a realtor. Liz came bright and early one morning. She took a look at our house and proceeded to give us a list of do's and don'ts. "Change the color of this room," "This coffee table and these pieces of furniture have to be stored in the garage."

"The cat and its litter box have to disappear when we are showing."

Who the heck does she think she is, bossing us around like this? It was my first encounter with this American phenomenon—the efficient, brash, and bossy female realtor—who knew exactly what the market wanted—and who would sell our house at the drop of a hat. Since then, I have acquired a deep respect for the hard-working and capable American realtors.

Six months later, on New Year's Day, we moved into a more spacious home, backing onto a golf course and man-made lakes. At last, I could enjoy the color green again with cottonwood trees in the backyard and a clear view of the Sandia mountains.

On the day of our move, we woke up to eight inches of snow. The family turned up to help, and they all pitched in. First, we had to clear the snow from the driveway. Once inside our new home, my two stepdaughters, Lydia and Maellen, and stepdaughter-in-law Martha set to covering the shelves and drawers with self-adhesive paper. I never had luck with that stuff—it would fold up on itself or stick to anything and everything other than the intended surface, and always askew. But the girls were experts, and soon had all the shelves and drawers covered. The men in the family carted in the furniture, and the older grandchildren helped too. In our exuberance, we even cleared the snow from a neighbor's driveway, who turned out to be a colleague of my stepson Jonathan. As an only child, I marveled at the communal spirit that prevailed among John's family members. Everyone chipping in and helping—it   was   indeed   "all   hands   on   deck." Our new home—new to us—was fairly large and sat on half an acre of land. There was a great deal to do because it was an older property and we bought it "as is." Coming from England, I did not fancy those spanky new, cookie-cutter, subdivision houses, where you can spit into the neighbor's yard. Older houses tend to have more character. John and I set about cleaning, clearing, and hiring workmen. It would take a couple of years, but it was a labor of love.

The yard also had been neglected. It was full of prickly pears, and cholla cacti. It was also my first encounter with the dreaded puncture weed and goatheads. At first, I admired the pretty yellow ground-hugging flowers, scattered around the yard, until those pretty flowers turned into nasty thorns. John told me that goatheads are the number one enemy of New Mexico gardeners. After a few nasty stabs from the little pests, I stopped walking barefoot around the house. It took a couple of years of persistent weeding before we became free of them.

In the US, urban sprawls are broken up every few miles, given new names with city status and covenants. To me, Rio Rancho was nothing but a suburb of Albuquerque. John called it the low-rent district. It served as a bedroom town since most residents commuted to Santa Fe or Albuquerque for work. Intel was the largest local employer and the only   industry.
Although there was a great deal to do around the house, we also needed to have a social life and cultivate friendships with like-minded empty-nesters. Domesticity has never been my métier, and I needed time away from house chores. The local library had just reopened after a two-year refurbishment. I sashayed in one morning and asked to join the book club. The chap behind the desk looked crestfallen.

"I'm sorry, but we haven't got one," he said.

"Really?"

"I tried. I asked my staff, but no one wants to do it."

I had hit on the chief librarian and his disappointment at not having a book club was obvious. Before engaging my mind, I blurted: "I'll do it." That's how I came to start the "Bookworms" book club at the

Esther Bone Library in Rio Rancho. From small beginnings, it grew and grew until we had to split into two groups. We read a variety of different genres of books. Each month we met to discuss, analyze, and comment before retreating to a nearby pub for more discussion and socializing. As it happened, our Tuesday meetings coincided with the local pub's ladies' night, which meant drinks and snacks at half price. Yay! Serendipity strikes again!

One of the books we read the first year was *The Guernsey Literary and Potato Peel Pie Society*. We decided to have a Potato Peel Pie meal at my house. I went on the internet to do some research and was surprised to find several "Potato Peel Pie" societies dotted all over the country, all offering helpful tips and pie recipes. What a hoot!

I primed a neighbor to burst in on our meeting, pretending he was a German officer. Mark played his role to perfection. He came with a megaphone and you could hear him all down the street announcing: "Achtung, Achtung. This ist the Geshshshtapo!! You have broken the curfew. All culprits must come out with their hands up." Of course, we invited him in and offered him a piece of potato peel pie, which, by the way, was delicious.

Another time we decided to have an Ethiopian meal after we had read *Cutting for Stone*. I bought the spices online and studied the recipes. We sat on cushions on the floor, Indian-Ethiopian style, eating delicious curries with naan bread.

It was through the book club I met Gwen. She joined early on, and we soon found that we had a great deal in common. She was also an avid reader, an artist, and had traveled extensively. She was a transplant from New York City. Her husband worked for the State Department, and they had spent many years overseas. By the time we met, she was widowed. We clicked right away. She became my go-to person whenever I encountered something unfamiliar. Her down-to-earth attitude and candor helped me navigate some of the unfamiliar customs and attitudes I encountered in the American Southwest.

I also joined the fledgling art group in Rio Rancho, which gave me the kickstart I needed to start painting again. I was asked to give a demo on Chinese brush painting—better known as Sumi-e in the United States. Soon, I began teaching this ancient art form at our local Hobby Lobby. I was busy making new friends and having fun at the same time. I also volunteered as a language tutor for a local literacy charity as well as helping out at a food bank. Not all these tasks and activities occurred at the same time, but they met my need for stimulation and interesting social interaction.

I asked Gwen whether she missed New York. "Hell, I do, but I can't afford to return to the East Coast. I burned my bridges behind me."

"John has said that too. Once you leave either coast, you can't go back unless you have lots of money."

"That's one reason they call New Mexico 'The Land of Entrapment' instead of the Land of Enchantment."

For some reason that comment sent shivers down my spine. The thought of being trapped in any way made me feel uncomfortable. There was a tone of finality in that statement.

CHAPTER EIGHT

AN INNOCENT ABROAD

As soon as we were married, John began the application process for me to become a permanent resident. It was a drawn-out ordeal involving endless forms, hefty fees, and then the long wait for Homeland Security. I was X-rayed and fingerprinted more times than Al Capone. Finally, Homeland Security summoned us for an interview.

On the appointed day, we arrived at the interview site—a large, imposing building near the airport. What surprised me most was the number of armed guards. Later, I learned that the building also served as a holding facility for people awaiting deportation. Coming from England, where police and security services do not routinely carry firearms, I found this daunting.

Soon, a uniformed femme formidable, wearing a sidearm, approached us. "Mr. and Mrs. Curran?"

"Yes."

"I'm Officer Garcia. Follow me!" she said, spinning on her heel. We followed her down a long, winding corridor.

Trying to lighten the mood, I whispered to John, "Just as well she's leading the way. I'd never find my way out of here. It's a labyrinth!"

"You can't get out of here without me! I have to let you out!" barked Garcia over her shoulder as she led us into a small interview room. She took her seat behind a large desk while we perched nervously on the chairs opposite.

"Now, these questions are for you, Mr. Curran," she began. I took that as my cue to keep silent until addressed.

"What's your wife's name?" she asked John.

"Which wife?" he replied.

She snapped her head up and glared at him. "How many do you have? Are you a bigamist?"

Her tone startled John. His late wife of 48 years had passed away just a year earlier, and we had brought documents related to her—birth certificate, marriage certificate, death certificate. No wonder he wasn't sure which wife she meant. From there, the interview went downhill. He couldn't recall my sons' birthdates and became increasingly flustered.

Having thoroughly disoriented my husband, she turned to me. "How and where did you meet?" she asked. "What are the names and ages of his children?" Fortunately, I knew.

Then she changed tack. "Now, Mrs. Curran. Are you a terrorist?"

"No!" What a ridiculous question. As if any terrorist would say yes.

"Do you know any terrorists?"

"No."

"Have you associated with any terrorists?"

"No."

"Are you, or have you ever been, a communist?"

"No! I wouldn't even know where to find the Communist Party in England."

"Are you, or have you ever been, a prostitute?"

"What?" Had I heard her right?

"Are you, or have you ever been a prostitute?" she repeated.

I was tempted to respond flippantly—Don't you remember Rodeo Drive when we had the same John?—but since my husband's name is John, I bit my tongue. The absurdity of the question made me giggle. Between chuckles, I managed to say, "I'm sorry, Officer Garcia, we didn't know what to expect. As you can see, we came completely unprepared." Like lambs to the slaughter.

The memory of that time in Harbin, North China, when I was mistaken for a Russian prostitute, flashed through my mind—but I wisely kept it to myself. Officer Garcia seemed to be on high alert already.

I sensed John growing angry. He was likely thinking: I'm a veteran. My ancestors came on the Mayflower. Don't speak to my wife like that! I gently placed my hand on his shoulder. "She's just doing her job," I whispered.

Perhaps she finally realized the elderly couple before her were neither terrorists nor prostitutes. Her tone softened. "I have to ask these questions." Then, as if still unsatisfied, she added, "I need to see more evidence of your wedding."

"Of course. You already have our marriage certificate."

"I want more. Photographs."

"We have letters, cards, and photographs," I said. "If you let us out of this maze, we'll return within the hour."

She agreed, leading us out once more, her gun holstered and hips swinging. We collected our things from the front desk, rushed home, gathered wedding invitations, cards, photographs, and a video, and returned to the Homeland Security building. After a brief inspection of our stash, she granted me my residency.

***

A couple of months after we were married, as we drove along Route 66, a strong, pungent smell filled the air. "What's that smell?" I asked.

"It's Hatch Chili time."

"It's what?"

"It's Hatch Chili being roasted. I love that smell," John said.

I had no idea what he was talking about. He explained that Hatch chili, grown in the southern town of Hatch, is the holy grail for New Mexicans who love the fiery vegetable. As the state's premier crop, harvested Hatch chili is distributed to retailers all over the state and beyond. The next time I went to the shops, I saw how the chili was roasted in big open-mesh barrels, churning over a gas burner while surrounded by salivating customers waiting to buy it in bulk—often enough to last all year. As I watched, I wondered about the spelling of chili, or chilli, or Chile. Chile, to me, is the country, and chili is the spice. In Europe, we usually spell it chilli. I'm afraid I'm not a chili aficionado, but the roasting smell was a reminder that summer was over and autumn was on the way. It was very New Mexico.

I was raised on the Mediterranean diet, while for John, the most exciting food was squash, in all shapes and sizes, clam chowder, comfort food, and anything with chocolate and oodles of sugar, betraying his New England roots. He had never tasted a gyro wrap or a mango before we met, and to this day he continues to call avocados artichokes. The infuriating thing about his diet is that he never puts on weight. It's a family joke that The Currans have two stomachs: one for food and one for dessert. I can vouch that's true. As I watch him eat, I put on weight––by osmosis. Over the years, he has graciously come to enjoy my cooking and lets me have free rein in the kitchen.

I enjoyed our big tribal potlucks. I introduced my new family and friends to the tastes of the Mediterranean, Asia, and the Middle East with my contributions of noodle salads, tabouli, souvlaki, and baklava—food they described as "exotic." They often asked for the recipes, and I was glad to oblige. But after listing the fifth or sixth ingredient, a glazed look on their faces told me that was the cut-off point. They would never make those dishes. Stuffed vine leaves and moussaka are great dishes, but too much work.

**

I lasted without home help for about six months until I was lucky to find a wonderful lady from Spain. Maria had been recommended by an acquaintance, and she eventually became more than our cleaner. She became a good friend.

Rio Rancho was known to have one of the best Senior Centers in the area. Tony, the cook, was at one time the chef at the Hyatt Tamaya Resort. Seniors came from far beyond our catchment area for his tasty $2 meals. On meatloaf day, the most popular meal, the dinner line was stacked 50 deep.

The Center also offered classes in computer studies, art, line dancing and a host of other activities. When I first suggested we lunch there, John responded: "I don't want to eat with a bunch of old farts."

"Well... we're old farts, so we should blend in nicely," I replied. Eventually, he overcame his reluctance. Most days we lunched there, and soon made new friends. We were pleasantly surprised to find a motley group of interesting people—retired or semi-retired engineers, educators, military, artists and other professionals. Many had lived full lives and had fascinating stories to tell. I wanted to put them all in a book—if I had time. Those stories and memories needed to be recorded. To my regret, I never made the time.

In the beginning, whenever people asked how we met, we were shy about owning up to internet dating. After a while, we overcame our reticence and 'fessed I was an "e-bride." The usual response was: "Oh, really? How interesting!" Sometimes we were asked for advice about internet dating. I guess it's never too late. Even old farts can dream of romance and a soul mate.

After a few years, I decided to apply for US citizenship. It was time. I majored in political science and worked for years in the world of current affairs and politics. I wanted to be more involved in my new country's life. An American friend jokingly said, "Now you can be one of us and complain." As a citizen, I could exercise my rights under the First Amendment—in fact all the amendments—which included complaining, criticizing and analyzing, and forming opinions. I could vote and be eligible for jury service, just like any other American. Vive la liberté.

It was not long before this new-found freedom got me into trouble. Naively I thought that in the land of the free one could exchange views and opinions on most topics, including politics. It happened quite unexpectedly when I helped out at a food bank in Albuquerque. While we were stocking the pantry shelves, I mentioned to another female volunteer how much I enjoyed the movies and commentaries of a certain Michael Moore. I liked his tongue-in-cheek iconoclastic approach to government, corruption, and Washington politics. Her initial reaction was to inform me that Michael Moore "is not a nice person." She tried hard to disabuse me of my admiration for Moore. When I told her that I thought he was an excellent journalist, and that perhaps more Americans should follow his lead, she angrily yelled, "If you don't like the way we do things here, then go back where you came from!"

Her comment was not only hurtful but left me perplexed. I had never encountered such rudeness. It was a vitriolic attack.

The next day, I called up my friend Gwen to tell her what happened. "I see," she said, and without pausing for breath, "you've encountered the ugly American."

"The what?"

"Haven't you seen the movie or read the book?"

"No."

"It's unfortunate that you've been attacked in this way. I consider it an attack. Some ignorant person who, most likely has never set foot outside her self-imposed comfort boundaries.

"She isn't ugly..."

"The term does not refer to looks but behavior and attitudes. It describes someone arrogant, narrow-minded, thoughtless, uneducated and rude." Gwen was on a roll. She continued, "I am often ashamed of my fellow countrymen. Their bigotry and ignorance gives us a bad rep, home and abroad. Did you say she worked at the food bank?"

"Yes, as a volunteer, like me, and she says she's a Christian."

"Spare me the hypocrisy of religion as a cover-up for bigotry and chauvinism."

Gwen was even more upset than I was. Her remarks got me thinking. I decided not to let the hurtful comments linger in my psyche. In the years that followed, I met several more "ugly Americans."

Every country has its mix of good and bad. Before I came to the United States the Americans I met abroad were mostly diplomats, journalists, and business people—well educated, well-traveled and well informed. Here, I saw a different mix. I had to take the rough with the smooth.

On another occasion, Gwen said: "Eventually you'll acquire the knack of sniffing out these idiots from a distance... they do give off a bad odor, and you'll learn to avoid them." Then she added: "Just look at their bumper stickers. Look at their behinds! That's where the shitty smell comes from!" She certainly had not lost her New York sense of humor. Like Michael Moore she was an iconoclast too.

At times, I wondered whether this ignorance of the wider world, outside the United States, had something to do with the dearth of international news in the local media. Admittedly the United States is a big country that generates a wealth of information, but state newspapers and television stations seldom report news from other states, unless it's something major. Parochialism and local sports are the main fodder for local media. The average reading level of local newspapers in the US is said to be that of 11th grade.

***

At times, I felt like a fish out of water. When a lady asked about a silk jacket I wore to church one morning, I told her: "It's from China. My tailor made it for me." She looked at me quizzically and repeated in a sarcastic tone, "Her tailor made it for her." That I came from a place where you can have a tailor make your clothes did not sit well with her. I was an innocent abroad. I could have explained that overseas, and in China in particular, this is quite common. But, I thought better of it. It was not my place to educate or inform her that there is another world out there, and probably it would be a waste of time.

Incidents like that, however, made me realize I had to be more tactful and careful when I spoke. This was a different environment from the one I was used to. Soon I learned not to talk in too much detail about my foreign experiences. After an initial "Where are you from?" the conversation often reverted to the more banal. Please don't tell me about your wonderful kids/wife/pets/grandkids. And don't tell me that Britain is a socialist country, just because we have a welfare system and a national health service. Gwen's words "Self-imposed comfort boundaries," often came to mind.

On the way back from the Senior Center one day, John told me it would be better not to mention that I had a cleaning maid.

"There were some odd looks exchanged among the women at our lunch table today when you mentioned your cleaner. In these parts, people don't have maids."

"So who helps them with the housework and the kids?" I said.

"No one. They do it themselves."

"How do they find the time?"

"They make time. That's all they do. They are homemakers and some homeschool their own kids. They don't work outside the home."

"But don't they get bored?"

"No . . . I don't think so."

I failed to understand how women with large families coped without help. I liked having a clean, welcoming home, but as I had so many interests and hobbies I did not want to devote most of my time to housework. I needed the stimulation of social interaction away from domestic chores.

Bed making was one example. After making the bed, I was exhausted. American beds are high. I needed a footstool just to climb into it. The European duvet did not exist in Albuquerque. Our California King had a bottom cover for the mattress, covered by a bottom sheet, and then a top sheet. Then came the comforter—which provided no comfort, because each time John turned he'd take it with him and leave me sans cover—followed by four pillows, a bedspread, and as if that wasn't enough, three or four additional decorative cushions on top. It took me about 15 minutes a day to make the bed and 10 minutes each evening to remove all the cushions and bed cover.

In search of a duvet and duvet cover, John took me to Linen 'n Things. The young assistant had no idea what a "duvet" or duvet cover was. My stepson's wife, Martha, came to the rescue. She had lived in England and spoke my language. She advised me to search the internet. Amazon came to the rescue. What a relief! Out went the blankets, top sheets, bedspreads, and half a dozen pretty little shiny, satiny, cushions. Making the bed these days is a breeze.

Homeschooling was also something I had not encountered before. It is not as prevalent in Europe as in the US. I'm not sure that it's even allowed in some countries. My stepdaughter Lydia, mother of eight, homeschooled her entire brood. I asked her how she coped. She smiled sweetly and told me that she enjoyed being a homemaker.

As a devoted wife and mother, she was determined to run her household along the lines of the movie *The Little House on the Prairie*, where years earlier she had a bit part as an extra. She and her kids dressed as if they still lived in that period. Somehow she found time to make her own cleaning products and toothpaste, distrusted microwave ovens, and did not use nonstick cooking pots or pans. She championed healthy eating and organic food products and worried that cancers were caused by chemicals in our food, soil, and atmosphere. How she found the time amazed me, with 10 people to feed each day. She was a good cook. I often asked for her recipes which she gladly shared.

But this came at a price. The children's schooling suffered. As a former teacher, I knew that without training it's impossible to teach eight kids, of different ages and abilities.

It wasn't long before I was asked to tutor the older homeschoolers and help with their English. One look at their textbooks and I was appalled. The print was too small, the books had no color or pictures, and were extremely boring. They were not child-friendly. I had seen better books in the slum schools of Hong Kong. I offered to teach vocabulary and etymology and give the kids spelling lessons to help them. I'd planned to give each child a diagnostic test to find their level of competence.

I was never taken up on my offer.

One day, while making a cake, I asked one of the homeschooled youngsters if she enjoyed learning about chemistry and weights and measures. She looked puzzled. Her older, teen brother asked, "What's chemistry?"

"It's one of the subjects you study with science. Like physics, biology, and chemistry"

"We don't do science."

"What? . . . How come?"

He had no idea. I looked at his mother who quickly interjected: "We have our own curriculum which we follow."

"But doesn't your curriculum offer the three basic science subjects for teens?" I said.

"We follow a very good program, it covers everything," she said defensively. I thought it best not to pursue the matter, but I put it on my mental "To Learn List" (TLL). Like in China, I kept my thoughts to myself.

I later met parents who had successfully homeschooled their children. They followed different curricula and did not keep their kids isolated. Many sent their teens to the local community college for extra lessons.

Sadly, my stepdaughter, Lydia, despite all her efforts and caution, died from an aggressive form of breast cancer a few days after her 56th birthday, leaving eight orphaned children and a grieving husband. The tragedy still reverberates with me, as it does for the family and all those who knew her.

There was an even bigger surprise for me when I asked another homeschooling mother where her daughters were planning to go to college. Her reply came swift and sharp.

"Oh, we don't send our girls to college."

What? It was like whiplash. Did I hear right? "Why?" I asked, still reeling.

"They are going to get married and have a family. They don't need college for that."

My father's words "Education is wasted on a woman" engulfed me like a tsunami of resurrected hurts, pain, and abuse. Half a century later I was again encountering the same attitude. Here, in the United States of America. In the 21st century! A nightmare come alive. This time a woman echoing those words.

"But, if they have the ability and the brains, why not send them to college?" I asked. "We don't believe in college education for our children," she said. The girls would live at home until they got married. Waiting for Prince Charming. And what if he never showed up? What if he wasn't so charming after all?

"But how are they going to survive in the world? How will they live without an education?" Again, all I got was a beatific smile.

"What if she never gets married, or the husband is incapacitated, or leaves or dies? Who is going to support her and any kids she may have?" I said.

"We are responsible for the way we raise our kids," she responded sharply. I took that as my cue to shut up. It was as good as saying: "Mind your own business. This does not concern you."

Still shocked, when I next met Gwen, I asked her point-blank how she felt about parents who refused to send their kids, and more specifically their girls, to college.

"Yes, I've encountered it before," she said.

"This goes against everything I believe in," I told her.

"They don't think like that. Fear and ignorance govern their thinking. And you're right about the females. They are deprived of a college education. They are primed to be good wives, mommies, and homemakers. It's a kind of brainwashing."

"What if they never get married?" I asked.

"Well . . . their primary role is to get married. If they don't get married they stay at home and take care of their parents or help raise younger siblings, nephews, and nieces."

I hoped that she might be wrong, but I had been told, in no uncertain terms, that college was not for girls. What bothered me most was that those girls were not given a choice.

In the land of the free, these girls were being deprived of the freedom to choose and to decide for themselves. Even worse, women were complicit in this brainwashing—women were to be homemakers, and men to be breadwinners.

After a while, as I settled in my new country I began to meet more people and make new friends. I realized that these attitudes were not the norm. Not all Americans homeschool their children or fail to send their daughters to college. When I asked them about this rigid gender divide, they were as surprised as I was. What I had encountered was a sub-culture.

***

Throughout history, when a certain section of society feels threatened, it resorts to "fight" or "flight" mode. When people withdraw and isolate themselves from the mainstream, sub-cultures emerge. With the advent of social media, the isolation need not always be physical. Interests, prejudices, and likes or dislikes are shared on Facebook, Blogs, Twitter, Instagram, and similar sites. I always thought that America was a country proud of being a melting pot, and proud of its diversity. Not quite so. At least this is what I was discovering in the Southwest. There were pockets of Hispanics, Anglos, and Asians. There were further sub-groups within each group. My neighbor, Roy, told me that his mother was proud of the fact that she was a direct descendant of the conquistadors. She spoke pure Castellano—Castilian Spanish—rather than Mexican Spanish. When I met John's friend, Arturo, he told me that he was not Mexican but Chicano. A term I had not heard before. The so-called melting pot seemed to contain elements that refused to meld. It's called diversity, but I sensed undercurrents flowing in opposite directions.

A recent debate on whether we should re-name Columbus Day and call it Indigenous People's Day reminded me of something I had learned in school, during a history lesson, when Miss Asher quoted the ditty:

"In Boston, the Lowells speak only to the Cabots

And the Cabots speak only to God."

In recent years, this polarization has created a chasm between Republicans and Democrats. I wonder if it can ever be bridged, much less eliminated. As a friend said: "I wish we could all be as we were the day after 9/11 when the whole country pulled together as one."

Do we need another 9/11 to bridge the gap? I hope not.

***

I was familiarizing myself with my surroundings and the culture of New Mexico. Was the rest of the country the same? As I met people who had lived or who had come from other states, I realized that there is a North-South, as well as an East-West divide. Nor is the South one uniform whole. Texas is different from Mississippi, and Alabama is very different from New Mexico or Arizona. Between East and West lies that vast geographical expanse, now referred to as the fly-over states.

Ken Burns and my husband are responsible for my education about the USA. John described his trips across the United States in a 1929 Model-A Ford. He recounted the hardships his family endured during the Great Depression. Ken Burns' documentaries helped bring John's memories to life with his series on the Rust Belt, Country Music, and Prohibition. They helped me understand the prevailing attitude of self-sufficiency, self-reliance, and self-help—a legacy of the time when pioneers traveled west in caravans, determined to conquer new land, brave hardships, and become self-sufficient. We don't need maids. We can manage our households.

It is also possible that this reluctance to hire cleaners stemmed, perhaps, from the period of slavery—some kind of generic, genetic guilt made it difficult for average middle-class families to hire maids, although finances also had a great deal to do with it.

John has this "I can fix it" attitude in full measure. I named him "Mr. Fix-it." No sooner did I point out something that needed a repair, than he was onto it. Home Depot was his favorite port of call, together with Lowes and Harbor Freight.

***

I was rather gratified to discover that I was not the only person who had never heard of New Mexico and did not know where it was. The monthly New Mexico magazine even carries a regular column entitled "One of our 50 is missing." It reports on stories of misunderstanding and ignorance about the whereabouts of New Mexico.

At times, when ordering online, I was told, "Sorry, we don't ship overseas." So I am not the only one who's never heard of New Mexico. At least my excuse is that I'm an Auslander. But now that I knew better, I was more than glad—eager in fact—to set the record right. I took great pleasure informing these ignoramuses that New Mexico is well and truly embedded into the US map, between Arizona and Texas. It is the state of the famous Hatch chili, the state where aliens reside in Roswell, and where the first atomic bomb was produced and tested. It's the state where Paul Allen and Bill Gates launched personal computers and Microsoft. It also has a town called Truth or Consequences. So there! At which point the poor creature at the other end of the line—phone or internet—got the message! Even some outsourced workers in Timbuktu got the message.

I quickly realized that in the Southwest public transport was not in the cards. A car was not a luxury, but a necessity. My UK driving license was good for six months, but I had two problems—I had never driven an automatic car, and I had to learn to drive on the "wrong" side of the road. We practiced in the K-Mart empty parking lot. My left foot kept looking for the clutch and my left hand searched for the shift stick! Eventually, I got the hang of it. The only vehicle I could not handle was John's truck. I did not have the confidence to handle that behemoth.

Driving around neighboring subdivisions, I noticed that the most prominent architectural feature of many houses was the garage—often double-doored. We lived on a long winding street, and I only saw my neighbors when their garage doors went up and they drove in or out.

There was no sense of community. Occasionally, when we both happened to be out in our respective yards, we exchanged polite inanities with our neighbors.

After we'd lived on that street for a few years, I noticed that our next-door neighbor was holding an estate sale. I love estate and garage sales, so I popped in to see what was on offer. Chatting to one of the women in charge, I asked where our neighbors were going. "Oh, just down the road. The house is too big for him," she said.

"Does Karen mind moving?" I asked.

"Karen's dead."

This was news to me. "When?"

"Three years ago. She just went to sleep and never woke up."

My surprise turned to astonishment. This couple had lived next door for 10 years and suddenly I was finding out that the wife had been dead for the past three! For some reason, I felt guilty. It was most peculiar. Later, I heard through the grapevine that she had committed suicide. I had seen her only a couple of times and hardly knew her, but her death left me nonplussed.

I blame automatic garage doors for this kind of alienation and isolation.

As with doughnuts, Americans don't content themselves with just one car, they need a second one. We had two vehicles—John's beloved truck and a little Scion. In America, every 16-year-old has a divine right to a driver's license and a car. Just take a look at high school parking lots.

Early on, I volunteered as an ESL (English as a Second Language) tutor for a local charity. Most of the clients were Spanish speakers. Many of the women wanted to learn English to get better jobs and help their kids with homework. Their ambition and high expectations reminded me of the parents whose children I had taught in Beijing. It was quite refreshing. They were so different from the homeschooling moms who refused to send their daughters to college. These new Americans were aware of the hardships and realities of life.

***

John and Gwen often tried to curb my tendency to be spontaneous and natural with people. I had to learn that upon meeting new people, you do a little dance, a pas de deux—a kind of mental negotiation to gauge the other person's attitude. Then you take a step back and let them approach you with the same intention. This goes back and forth in the guise of polite conversation, exchanging banalities: "safe" subjects such as the weather, family history, kids, jobs, homes, and food ad nauseam. Two steps forward, one step back. Sometimes it's one step forward and two steps back. Ouch!

Gwen advised: "Don't discuss politics or religion with people you don't know well. This is not Europe or England. Americans can be very defensive about their beliefs and politics. We think our country is the best in the world. We call it exceptionalism."

I had encountered this same attitude in China, India, Britain, and several other countries. America was not unique in thinking that it is the best, most exceptional country in the world. Jingoism and populism were two main reasons for wars. Could this be why the United States was always at war, ever since 1776? There's hardly been a decade when the US has not been at war, either overtly or covertly.

I was beginning to appreciate Ruth's warning in London: "The only Americans you will have anything in common and enjoy socializing with are those who have lived and traveled abroad, with similar experiences and interests as you."

In England, one can discuss politics, religion, and sex with friends and family, even with strangers. We might not always agree. There were heated discussions and arguments, but in the end, people agreed to disagree without the vitriol and finger-pointing I experienced in the US. And since guns are not legally available, Brits don't shoot each other when they argue. Heated debates were safe and intellectually stimulating—at least for me.

***

Like most households, we were at the receiving end of unsolicited calls. Every Saturday morning, a regular caller asked for a Mr. Bradsher. I think he may have had the same telephone number as us. In the end, I assured the caller that "Mr. Bradsher was sadly no longer with us." "He's dead," I said. It worked. The calls stopped. Mr. Bradsher, whoever and wherever you are, if you are reading this, please forgive me.

Santa Fe, the capital of New Mexico, known also as The City Different, has a unique style and is known for art and its opera season. The concha belts with their silver and turquoise stones, the flared skirts with leather tassels, the adobe homes, and the mystique around Georgia O'Keeffe add to the allure of the City Different. My cousin Don, a classical music fan, informed me that Santa Fe is the Glyndebourne of America, which deflected somewhat his fears about my moving to the US.

Since we lived about an hour's drive from Santa Fe, I could explore the art galleries on Canyon Road and wander around the Plaza. Artisans on Cerrillos Road became a favorite haunt, where I purchased some of my art supplies. Not far from Artisans, I discovered a wonderful eatery called Jumbo that served East African and Caribbean food.

I think Santa Fe was more impressed with itself than I was with it. It holds the title of being the oldest capital in the USA. Good to know if you play Trivia. Most jewelry shops in the Plaza are run by Middle Easterners. Genuine local jewelry is available from Native Americans who lay out their wares under the shade of the covered walkway around the Plaza.

***

With so many grandchildren to our credit, we were often invited to their graduations. Americans take the ritual of graduation to new heights. Kids graduate from play school, from kindergarten, from elementary school, from middle school, from high school, and college. Caps and gowns are made for all shapes, sizes, and age groups. One of our granddaughters' sons recently "graduated" from preschool to "proper" school, and Facebook displayed plenty of photographs, posted by his proud mom. As in most such cases, there was plenty of food to go around. Don't Americans ever have an event or celebration without food?

While I can understand proud parents' desire to show off their kids, I was wondering if all this hoorah—marking every progression of a child's life—might be creating, once again, another social divide. I was mindful of those parents who struggle to raise a family and put food on the table. They'd find it hard to emulate all this extravagance. All the showing off would surely make them feel guilty because they could not afford to do the same.

According to my friend Linda, this is something new. "In my days we had only a couple of graduations, celebrating transition to high school, end of high school, and then college," she said. "Now it's gone crazy. Anything to make a fast buck. Marketing is exploiting parents big time."

"Well, that's capitalism. Isn't it?" I said.

"Capitalism is for those who can afford it. Have you seen how aggressive marketing has become around kids? Not just birthdays and Christmas... now we have all this trashy stuff for sale for baby showers, gender reveal showers, wedding showers, and Halloween. And it's very clever. They make you feel you're a bad parent if you don't spend, spend, spend on your kids."

"But it's up to parents, surely, whether they want to be sucked in by all this advertising?"

"Yes and no. It's become a fad and very competitive. Parents vie to give the most extravagant and showy party."

"And those who can't?"

"They're made to feel second-class or inadequate."

I had noticed the same trend in China, with its increased prosperity, as well as in the UK. Marketing gurus had discovered the Achilles' Heel of parents and grandparents.

***

New Mexico has a magnetism difficult to describe. A poor state, and sparsely populated, New Mexico's charm and attraction are unique. People are drawn to its big wide-open vistas, laid-back pace of life, blue skies, and healthy climate. The cost of living is much lower than on either coast, and taxes are reasonable. The mountains offer great skiing in winter, and in summer, a welcome escape from the heat. It is awash with beautiful Native American, and Spanish art, weaving, jewelry, and pottery.

During the Christmas season, New Mexico turns into a wonderland lit by thousands of luminarias (called farolitos in Santa Fe) that glow in the night, gracing front yards, ancient monuments, and public places—a veritable fairyland that draws visitors from around the country.

When I first arrived, I noticed the preponderance of the color brown—brown adobe houses, brown sun-scorched earth, and the muddy brown of the Rio Grande. But when monsoon rains soak the dry soil, dormant flower seeds sprout into a riot of colors, just as I had seen in the Gobi desert in Mongolia. The monotony of browns is broken by the golden colors of Aspens and Cottonwoods. I have come to love these colors and often use them in my weaving and artwork.

Indeed, the Land of Enchantment inspired people like Georgia O'Keeffe, Mabel Dodge Lujan, Alfred Stieglitz, Ansel Adams, and R.C. Gorman. It is said that Los Alamos has more PhD scientists than Silicon Valley. New Mexico is also a favorite location for filming, boosted by state grants to movie companies. *Breaking Bad*, the TV series filmed in Albuquerque, put New Mexico on the map.

There is a saying in New Mexico that if you live in Albuquerque, you are bound to have house guests the first week of October. Several events draw visitors to the state—the Albuquerque International Hot-Air Balloon Festival, the Greek Fiesta, and the Taos Wool Festival. All take place during the first full week in October. There is hardly a room to be had in any hotel, motel, or inn.

I love the Balloon Fiesta, and John and I have introduced several house guests to this event. On the opening day, always a Friday, we drag them out of bed before dawn to attend the mass ascension. In the dark and before sunrise, the balloons, still tethered, are filled with gas. Like red glowing baubles, they rise to an upright position, their gondolas ready to receive passengers. This is the Dawn Patrol—an amazing and beautiful sight. Suddenly, the sun breaks through, lighting up their beautiful colors as they soar heavenward, literally hundreds of them.

Weeks before the Fiesta, we see hot-air balloons in the sky. I knew when one was flying low over our home by the "whoosh, whoosh" sound as gas was released into the balloon to make it rise.

The same weekend as the Balloon Fiesta, the Greek community holds its annual Greek Festival in downtown Albuquerque—my annual homage to Greek lamb and genuine Greek food. The folk dancing was always wonderful. I marveled at how the young dancers learned the complicated steps—danced in a chain—of Kalamatianos, Sirtaki, Zembekiko, and other traditional dances.

Also, that same first weekend in October, the annual Wool Festival is held in Taos. On one such visit, I came away with my first rigid-heddle loom. Before I knew it, I had joined Las Arañas, the Albuquerque weavers and spinners group, where I was soon surrounded by experienced weavers willing to share their expertise and help me learn the techniques of tapestry weaving. They welcomed me as a beginner and were patient as I took my first baby steps in this ancient and noble craft. I had some wonderful teachers in Nancy Wohlenberg and Mary Colton. John was also instrumental in teaching me how to maintain the right tension and how to warp my loom. We now share a hobby, and I can admire and understand the skill and effort he puts into his weaving, on a larger, more complex loom. He organized a wonderful weaving show at the Rio Rancho Inn with many renowned weavers taking part. There was a great variety of styles, ranging from very modern, including Susan Klebanoff's amazing three-dimensional wall hangings, to the Navajo and Rio Grande traditional weaving patterns. The owner told us it was the best show he had ever had at his place.

I grew to love and enjoy New Mexico and all it had to offer, but there was one drawback for us. The mile-high altitude was becoming a problem for John. After eleven years in the Land of Enchantment, it was time to get down to sea level and enjoy the soft breezes of the Pacific. It was a toss-up between leaving our family support group behind or enjoying a better and healthier lifestyle. The nomad in me was ready to move on.

CHAPTER NINE

CALIFORNIA HERE WE COME

San Diego had been in our crosshairs for some time. In 2012, we spent Thanksgiving in the downtown area, close to the Gas Lamp District. We decided we liked it enough to buy a second home there, for breaks away from the high desert. Southern California (SoCal) is the Mediterranean of the US, in both climate and flora. During our search, we discovered the "Jewel in the Hills," the City of La Mesa, in San Diego County. We liked its main street with its village character, its antique shops, the Friday farmers' market, numerous restaurants and its lack of pretentiousness. It's like a lady with a blue rinse when the Jacaranda trees are in full bloom. The city center had just been given a major facelift and was determined to keep its village look.

The sale of my London house made the purchase of a second home possible. Each time I visited England's metropolis, I was struck by its overcrowding, dirt, pollution, noise, and tired look. House prices were astronomical, and the steep rise in the cost of living persuaded me it was time to sell. A Chinese investor from Singapore bought my house. I wonder whether he was one of the wealthy Chinese depicted in the movie Filthy Rich Asians. I'll never know.

At the time, the exchange rate between the US dollar and the English pound was in my favor. When the large sum of money swelled my US bank account, I suddenly became a person of substance in the eyes of my local branch. No longer invisible, every time I went to the bank, I was warmly greeted: "Oh, hello, Mrs. Curran. How are you today? Would you like to see the manager?" and I was ushered into the manager's office. I no longer had to stand in line with the other customers. The manager tried hard to convince me that I needed to consult one of their financial advisors and offered me several investment opportunities. The financial advisors would even pay a house call to discuss my options. Welcome to the Land of Milk and Money. Capitalism and plutocracy are genial bed follows.

Recalling my mother's advice of years ago, I decided to invest in bricks and mortar rather than shares. This is how we were able to buy a holiday condo in San Diego County. John and I, as well as family and friends, enjoyed vacationing there. The more days we spent in La Mesa, the more we liked it. When the time came for us to leave the Land of Enchantment, the decision was easy. California, here we come!

Relocating and downsizing are mammoth tasks. The kind of job I prefer to leave on the back burner. However, we had little time for prevarication. We needed to move for health reasons while we still had the energy and strength to do it. We were running out of a lifetime. In May 2017, after several months of backbreaking sorting, packing, throwing out "stuff," and organizing an estate sale, we moved to San Diego.

For John, the move was bitter-sweet. He had spent nearly 30 years in New Mexico, and his family was firmly entrenched there—children, grandchildren, and great-grandchildren. But his lungs suffered from lack of oxygen in Albuquerque's mile-high altitude. Relocating to California, he was coming back full circle to the state where he was born.

The gypsy in me looked forward to the change and getting my feet wet walking along the sandy shores of the Pacific. Memories of my childhood growing up in Cyprus flooded in. No wonder Southern California is known as the Mediterranean of America.

Our backyard in La Mesa is brimming with passion flowers, bougainvilleas, hibiscus, succulents, geraniums, and cacti. During morning walks with Maisie, our Old English Sheepdog, I can reach out and pick figs, pomegranates, lemons, and oranges that spill over fences onto the sidewalk. Our next-door neighbor's tree is happy to shed its avocados in our yard. Sipping a cup of coffee or a glass of wine on our patio, I watch hummingbirds hover over the fuchsia, Monarch butterflies flit around the passion flowers, and our resident squirrels hop along the fence and jump from branch to branch.

We are still exploring, discovering, and enjoying all that our town and area have to offer. John has discovered the local Home Depot and is happy with his many projects. La Mesa boasts an active artists' group— The Foothills Art Association—and its own gallery. Most amenities are within walking distance—church, my creative writing group, post office, library, police station, and a couple of supermarkets. The San Diego Watercolor Society is twenty minutes away by car.

**

I was surprised to discover that I experienced greater culture shock coming to America than when I lived in China. Possibly because I did not expect it. Having traveled and lived in so many different countries, I thought I'd be able to adapt and fit in easily. Oh boy! Was I in for a surprise.

The Americans I met now were unlike those I had met overseas––the diplomats, businessmen, and journalists.

I was now meeting the real meat and potatoes of the country. Rough diamonds who will bring you meals, give you the coat off their backs—salt of the earth—honest, hardworking people. The kind you can always rely on, and whose friendship I have come to appreciate and value. My father's warning "to trust no one" was being eroded by the kindness shown to me by so many people throughout my life.

So why did I suffer culture shock moving to the US? Primarily because the Southwest is of itself a special place. Unique. Several family members and friends told me that they too had found it difficult to adjust to New Mexico when they moved there from the East Coast. If they had problems adjusting, then my culture shock is understandable. Normal. I am normal. It's the strangeness around me that isn't.

"You'll get used to it, eventually," I was told. Meanwhile, I was encountering various belief systems—social, political, and economic—that were new to me. Some left me perplexed, some amused, and some questioning.

I was surprised to find that begging is prevalent and, in fact encouraged. I don't mean the homeless, or "signers," who stand on street corners, but those who ask for money through an online epidemic of GoFundMe accounts. A custom I have encountered only in the US. Need money for your kids, for medical bills, to pay a debt, to bury your spouse, to go on holiday? Set up a GoFundMe account and watch the money pour in. Cynical as this sounds, the GoFundMe accounts do speak to kind hearts and generosity. Many requests are worthy, and I have personally contributed to a few. I was upset to see friends and their families denied medical cover for pre-existing conditions. I was saddened and angry to see children and adults denied life-saving drugs by so-called non-profit medical insurance companies. These are the people who are forced to rely on charity through GoFundMe accounts. A large part of credit card debt is due to medical bills. Collection companies deal mostly with those who cannot afford to pay their medical bills.

In a consumer society, the more consumers consume, the better the economy. Cars are parked in the driveway so the garage can provide storage space for all that extra stuff we accumulate—discarded furniture, toys, and boxes filled with Christmas, Thanksgiving, Easter, Fall, and Spring decorations. Perhaps also a workbench with tools for all the DIY jobs and honey-do lists. Despite the existing hoard, each season beckons through newspaper ads, TV and billboards, "Come and buy! It's Black

Friday in August, Beat the Crowds." The shops are dressed in green for St. Paddy's Day, chocolate bunnies abound at Easter, scary stuff for Halloween, and inflatable Santa Clauses and reindeer for Christmas. All subliminal messages to part us from our money.

I asked a Costco manager why they didn't label their aisles— after I had wasted 10 minutes trying to find the maple syrup. "Oh, that'll never happen," he said. "The idea is to get you to walk around and buy more."

It takes an iron will to escape that Siren voice that beckons us to buy, buy, buy. No wonder Odysseus asked his men to tie him to the main mast and stuffed wax in his sailors' ears. He knew they could not resist their calls.

Nothing succeeds like excess. Hyperbole and superlatives abound: best, greatest, most blessed, exceptional, most democratic, most free, most cool, most generous and best price. Understatements are rare in a country whose very core is consumer manipulation with clever marketing.

Excess is to be expected in the wealthiest country in the world, but with excess comes waste. A recent PBS (Public Broadcasting Station) documentary stated that if Americans saved 15 percent of food they waste at home, it could feed an additional 25 million people. I am amazed by the huge portions served at restaurants. Meanwhile, there are people who survive from paycheck to paycheck, and many who are jobless, or homeless.

I admire the number of caring, kind and generous people with a social conscience who reach out and help as best they can. Lacking a social welfare system, this country has relied on individuals to do its job––to feed, care, and succor those in need. At the same time, I continue to be surprised that every time I suggest that it is the responsibility of the State to take care of all its citizens, including the marginalized, I am told:

"We don't want a nanny state" or "we don't need government involvement." This strong spirit of independence may be a remnant of early pioneer days when people lived at subsistence levels. But in an established democracy, with all its accumulated wealth, it is shameful that a large number of people sleep on the streets, vast numbers are without medical care, and even greater numbers of people work hard all their lives yet remain broke.

The various myths that abound also contributed to my culture shock. One such is the belief that anyone on benefits or welfare is a lazy freeloader. With a wide brushstroke, those receiving help are brushed aside from one's social conscience. Another myth is that the wealth of the one percent trickles down to the rest of us. There may be some truth in the belief that in addition to jobs, big corporations provide opportunities. But, it is the sweat and labor of its employees—from the janitor to the manager—that creates the one percent, and money does not always trickle down.

Another myth is that America is a classless society, and if you work hard, you will rise above the heap, both economically and socially, and attain the American Dream, supposedly available to all. But for most who fail to achieve the American Dream, it is an American Nightmare. Despite their hard work, many remain below the poverty line, isolated and marginalized. In a capitalist society where everyone is obsessed with wealth, poverty is considered something shameful. Still, another myth maintains that the poor can pull themselves up by their bootstraps. As if they had a choice.

The front cover of TIME magazine, dated September 24, 2018, displayed a picture of a middle-aged woman with the caption: "I have a master's degree, 16 years of experience, work two extra jobs, and donate blood plasma to pay the bills. I'm a teacher in America." Inside the issue was a long feature on the plight of teachers right across America.

These myths and beliefs help me understand why Americans do not take long vacations like their European counterparts. It explains why they are stressed out, and why they work long hours at jobs they do not particularly enjoy. Why they do not have national health care—considered a basic human right in most developed countries? Why they do not have maternity, paternity, or sick leave—also considered basic human rights in most civilized and developed countries. I've often been told: "If I lose my job I have no medical cover." So they put up with stressful and at times dangerous jobs, bad bosses, and poor working conditions. Even the well-organized auto workers unions could not prevent Motown (Detroit) from becoming Ghost Town.

Plutocracy in the US has its Russian equivalent in the oligarchs, and in China in the Party elites.

So why am I surprised that the United States isn't any different? I don't know. Or, perhaps I do. It's because WE ARE BETTER THAN THAT! But are we?

Before some "ugly American" reading all my misgivings and comments utters the ugly words: "If you don't like it here, then why don't you go back where you came from?" let me tell you some of the many things I really like and enjoy in the US. First and foremost is its people. The many wonderful, gracious, kind, and uplifting people I have come to know and call family and friends. Whenever there is a national or international disaster, Americans are the first to respond with help. I like the fact that many Americans are faithful churchgoers, and that people, from all religions and denominations, can worship in freedom and peace, that secularism has not snuffed out Christianity.

I like the respect shown to the flag, and that the Constitution is the highest law in the land. I like the respect shown to the military, even though I may not approve of some of the nation's current military engagements. I like the spirit of compassion, which enables Americans to see the need in others and help the many support and self-help groups––neighbors helping neighbors, mothers helping mothers, and charities reaching out to those in need.

I like the way children, at least in our family, are taught to be polite and address their elders as "sir" and "ma'am" and be respectful. I like the fierce spirit of independence that says "Yes I can." I like the fact that the family continues to remain strong and valued while accepting the rights of those who choose alternative lifestyles. I like the custom of potlucks where everyone brings a dish to share. I like the enthusiasm and participation generated by each small town when marking some anniversary with a parade—be it Mother Goose, Flag Day, or the Fourth of July.

Given the right conditions, there are opportunities for advancement, both economic and social. But most of those are beyond one's control. They include race, gender, education, geography, and background.

As a US citizen, I'm proud to say that I'm a citizen by choice, and not by accident of birth. I rest my case.

***

EPILOGUE

I left China in 2005, leaving the door ajar. I did not want to burn my boats behind me. One can't foresee the unpredictable, but I knew I could easily find work and settle back into my comfortable expat lifestyle if I wanted to return.

A year later, in 2006, all thoughts of returning to Beijing were scuppered by e-Harmony and John Curran. How we met is already recorded in this memoir. He came, he saw, he conquered. Instead of returning to China, I ended up in New Mexico, married to a New Englander whose ancestors were among the early colonizers of the New World. I took on the Davidson clan's tartan. I also became a US citizen. As I said before, I am a US citizen by *choice* and not by accident of birth.

Ten years later, in 2015, I returned to the People's Republic as part of a delegation with the Albuquerque Chamber of Commerce. What I found was a country transformed – more skyscrapers, an expanded subway system, wider roads, and a faster pace of life. The once-bustling Olympic Village in Beijing now stood deserted. Cars had replaced bicycles; hundreds of vehicles jostled for space, spewing fumes into an already polluted atmosphere. Visibility that day was reduced to about eight feet. Only the foolhardy and suicidal rode bicycles. High-speed trains zipped through sleek stations, and multilane expressways carved through the city. I canceled plans to visit old haunts and ducked into a drugstore to buy a face mask, just like during SARS. China had surged forward in nearly every sector – economic, military, political, and social.

The country is birthing home-grown billionaires faster than the USA. Once a meritocracy, China has now become a plutocracy, still governed by a communist regime. Deng Xiaoping's motto, "To be rich is glorious," has become the soul of China.

I lived through the outbreak of SARS in 2003, through the denials and cover-ups by Chinese officials pretending it did not exist and their many fake assurances that we were safe. How I survived is also recorded in this memoir. Sixteen years the same virus, now known as Covid-19, sent the world into panic and lockdowns. It left in its wake millions dead, suffering, and grieving. And it hasn't finished with us yet. This time, I took it seriously and followed the guidelines and precautions necessary to protect myself and my family. It was interesting to note that the Chinese Government used the same tactics of denial and pretense it did back in 2003 with SARS. It's a shame that some of our Government officials did the same and did not take timely action to save lives.

***

Home is now the United States of America. After years of wandering, my life's journey has brought me to the Western Hemisphere. The patchwork is nearly complete. The little girl who once cried herself to sleep, hoping a rich uncle would rescue her, has finally found refuge with Uncle Sam. He's not perfect—but then, neither is she. He welcomed her with warmth and affection, and over time, they've grown comfortable with each other.

Looking back, I see now that those early years of suffering were my training ground—the refiner's fire that gave me the strength to face future trials. I am grateful for family, friends, shelter, and happy memories with Jadie. These are privileges I don't take for granted.

***

In the ongoing treadmill of life, what hacks call "hatches, matches, and dispatches," I feel I am now nearing the "dispatches" section. I have lived life to the full, navigated roadblocks, pitfalls, twists, and turns. Most of my encounters have been enriching. I learned to live with the consequences of my and other people's actions.

It has been an interesting journey. Memories of Cyprus, Hong Kong, China, England, New Mexico, and now San Diego provide the fabric I have stitched together to form this tapestry of my life. It is still a work in progress.

Writing gurus advise that the end of a story should dazzle the reader and end on a high note. Mine is a quiet note.

I have had several crescendos, fortissimos, reprises, and syncopations in my life. I've had minors and majors and a few false starts. Now, it's time to sit back and enjoy the scent of jasmine, plumeria, and orange blossoms.

There remains just one small patch left to complete the whole. So far, it's been an extraordinary journey.

© **Nora Curran**

Jadie and Nora

BBC Monitoring Service at Caversham Park 1943-2018

NOTES AND SOME EXPLANATORY INFORMATION

CHAPTER ONE - Once Upon a Time . . .

1. Cyprus is the Easternmost island in the Mediterranean. It was conquered by the Phoenicians, the Persians, the Ptolemys, the Greeks and the Turks. It gave its name to copper and the cypress tree. Its history goes back to Paleolithic times. It was a British colony at the time of my birth. Cyprus gained its independence in 1959.

2. Galathea and Pygmalion first mentioned in Greek mythology. Pygmalion was a renowned Greek sculptor. His most famous and beautiful statue was that of a woman, Galathea. It was so beautiful he fell in love with it and was heart-broken that the cold marble could not reciprocate. He prostrated himself before his creation and sobbed night and day. The gods on Olympus took pity on him and blew life into the statue. Galathea and Pygmalion inspired George Bernard Shaw's novel "Pygmalion" and this in turn inspired the movie "My Fair Lady"

3. Clytemnestra and her daughter Iphigenia are mentioned in Greek mythology and the Trojan War. They both feature in the plays of Euripides and Aeschylus.

4. A hope chest, also called dowry chest, cedar chest, trousseau chest or glory box is a piece of furniture traditionally used to collect items such as clothing and household linen, by unmarried young women in anticipation of married life.

5. Smyrna was a Greek city founded in antiquity located on the Aegean coast of Anatolia, today's Turkey. Since 1930, the modern city located there has been known in English as Izmir.

6. Classics Illustrated is an American comic book/magazine series featuring adaptations of literary classics such as Les Miserables, Moby Dick, Hamlet and The Iliad. Created by Albert Kanter, the series began publication in 1941 and finished its first run in 1971, producing 169 issues.

CHAPTER TWO - Breaking Free

1. The story was fictionalized in a movie "Scandal" in 1989.

2. Ahmadou Babatoura Ahidjo was the first President of Cameroon, holding the office from 1960 until 1982. Ahidjo played a major role in Cameroon's independence from France as well as reuniting the French and English-speaking parts of the country.

3. When the Normans conquered Britain in 1066, William the Conqueror ordered one of the most thorough surveys of England and part of Wales. This was hand drawn and hand written on parchment, and fragments of it exist to this day. It is called the Domesday Book. The survey showed all the existing hamlets, towns, parishes, counties, estates, rivers and woodlands. William did this to help him tax his new subjects and their estates.

4. "BBC Monitoring" is a division of the British Broadcasting Corporation (BBC), which monitors, and reports on mass media worldwide. Until 2017 it was based in Caversham, outside the town of Reading in the county of Berkshire. It has a number of overseas bureaux. BBC Monitoring selects and translates information from radio, television, press, news agencies, and the Internet from 150 countries in more than 70 languages. Reporting produced by the service is used as open-source intelligence by elements of the British government and commercial customers. The BBC announced in July 2017 that it planned to sell the site at Caversham Park and move its offices to London.

5. An Orangery is a glazed structure attached to a stately home and acts as a greenhouse for tropical trees and other exotic plants. They were fashionable in the 17th to the 19th centuries.

6. The Equal Pay act was passed in 1970 and the Sex Discrimination Act in 1975, in the UK.

7. The British Crown Colony of Hong Kong consisted of several islands, the largest called Victoria where we lived, including the Kowloon Peninsula, as well as part of the New Territories north of Kowloon.

8. Typhoon is the name given to hurricanes in the Pacific. It is a Chinese word meaning "big wind." They usually start around the Philippine Archipelago and move northward with increasing speed.

CHAPTER THREE - Hong Kong

1. The Repulse Bay occupies the site of the former colonial-style Repulse Bay Hotel (1920-1982).The hotel was renowned for its British architectural style. During World War II, the hotel was used as a stronghold and a hospital by the British forces. Royalty and celebrities who found refuge at the hotel include writers George Bernard Shaw and Noël Coward. Actor Marlon Brando was a guest in the 1950s. Spain's Crown Prince Juan Carlos and Crown Princess Sofia spent their honeymoon there.

2. The Westminster system is a parliamentary system of government developed in the United Kingdom and exported to the colonies. In Hong Kong the Letters Patent formed the constitutional basis of government.

3. Feng Shui or fengshui, also known as Chinese geomancy is a pseudoscience originating from China, which claims to use energy forces to harmonize individuals with their surrounding environment. The term *feng shui* literally translates as "wind-water" in English.

The feng shui practice discusses architecture in terms of "invisible forces" that bind the universe, earth, and humanity together, known as *qi*. (Pronounced "she.") Before any structure was built, a geomancer would be asked to find the most propitious siting for the way the building should face, and the placement of doors and windows. Once he gave his approval and instructions then the construction could begin. Historically, feng shui was widely used to orient buildings—often spiritually significant structures such as tombs, but also dwellings and other structures—in an auspicious manner.

4. The inclusion of Chinese customary law, alongside the law of Hong Kong, has provided a snapshot of the customs and practices of the people of Hong Kong before its time as a British colony. These customs and practices preserved in the law of Hong Kong are part of the cultural heritage of China. It dealt with marriage and divorce among the Chinese residents, polygamy and concubines, which had already been eliminated from the People's Republic of China. Mao had liberate the women of China, but the customs and traditions of feudal times still lingered with overseas Chinese in places like Hong Kong, Macao, Malaysia, and Singapore.

5. An expatriate (often shortened to expat) is a person residing in a country, other than their native country. In common usage, the term often refers to professionals, skilled workers, or artists taking positions outside their home country, either independently or sent abroad by their employers, which can be companies, universities, governments, or non-government organizations. However, the term 'expatriate' is also used for retirees and others who have chosen to live outside their native country, eg. Americans living in Mexico or Costa Rica.

6. The Treaty of Nanking in 1842 established the five treaty ports: Shanghai, Canton, Ningpo, Fuchow, and Amoy (Xiamen). The following year the Chinese and British signed the Treaty of Bogue, which added provisions for extraterritoriality and most-favored nation status to Britain.

7. Hong Kong island consisted of three levels: sea level, the mid-levels and the Peak. One could either drive up to the Peak or take the funicular train there and enjoy panoramic views of the island and the harbor.

8. From the late 1980s to date, this dynamic has changed: the One-Child policy which came into force in China in 1979, Mao's legislation giving equal rights to women and Deng Shao Ping's Open Door to economic prosperity, were all contributing factors. Today the One-China policy is not strictly enforced.

9. Many other ancient civilizations had concubines, but in China it prevailed well into the 20th century. Today it still exists under its new name: human trafficking. Polygamy still exists in some cultures.

10. Kowloon Walled City was a largely ungoverned, densely populated settlement in Kowloon City in Hong Kong. Originally it was a Chinese military fort. By 1990, the Walled City contained 50,000 residents within its 6.4-acre borders. From the 1950s to the 1970s, it was controlled by local triads and had high rates of prostitution, gambling and drug abuse.

11. Later, Sue told me that she too had experienced the same feelings at an earlier meeting, and had left Mary Baker Eddy's church.

12. SAVAK was the Shah's secret police.

13. This was indeed the beginning of the "troubles" and the civil war in Lebanon which was to last several decades and rip the country apart. It is still ongoing today.

CHAPTER FOUR - Return to Blights

1. "Blighty" is an informal and typically affectionate term for Britain or England.

2. Broadmoor Common in West Devon is one of the few remaining wilderness areas in England. It has miles and miles of hiking trails, hills, valleys, lakes and springs, and is sparsely dotted with small towns and inns. A scary wilderness for an 8-year old to be lost.

3. The People's Republic of Mongolia is an independent land-locked country between China to the South and Russia to the north. Not to be confused with Inner Mongolia which is in the People's Republic of China.

4. A libation is a ritual pouring of a liquid, or grains such as rice, as an offering to a god or spirit, or in memory of the dead. It was common in many religions of antiquity and continues to be offered in cultures today, especially among Mongolian and Tibetan Buddhists. During our visit, the Mongolian hosts simply flicked a few drops of the drink into the air.

5. Throughout, I have used other variants for China, including, Middle Kingdom and Cathay or the People's Republic of China (PRC).

CHAPTER FIVE - China

1. The Hukou System. The system itself is more properly called "*huji*", and has origins in ancient China. *Hukou* is the registration of an individual in the system. A household registration record officially identifies a person as a resident of an area. The central government's efforts to contain migration has been a major factor in the rapid development of the Chinese economy. Their tight check on migration into urban areas has helped prevent the emergence of a number of problems faced by many other developing countries. A hukou can also refer to a family register.

2. *China Daily*, established in 1981, is the only national English-language newspaper in China. The average daily circulation is more than 200,000, one-third of which is abroad in more than 150 countries and regions. It is owned by the Communist Government.

3. *Hutong* are narrow alleys with courtyard houses called *Siheyuan*. Their history can be traced back to more than 800 years, when Beijing established its status as the capital city. As a kind of traditional Chinese relic, Siheyuan represents the capital's architectural style.

4. Jean Piaget, Swiss psychologist. Developed theory of cognitive development and knowledge, espoused by Western educationists.

5. The British Council is the UK's international organization for cultural relations and educational opportunities. It promotes knowledge and understanding between the people of the UK and other countries.

6. *Laowai* is the Mandarin pronunciation/transliteration of 老外 (pinyin: lǎowài, lit. "old foreign"), an informal term or slang for "foreigner" or non-Chinese national, usually neutral but possibly impolite or negative in some circumstances.

CHAPTER SIX - China Visitors

1. A Karst landscape is made of limestone which has been eroded by dissolution, producing ridges, towers, fissures and sinkholes.

2. Ethnic minorities in China are the non-Han Chinese population in China. China officially recognizes 56 ethnic minority groups within China in addition to the Han majority. As of 2010, the combined population of officially recognized minority groups comprised 8.49% of the population of mainland China. They have their own customs, religion and dress, but they are Chinese citizens.

3. This was in 2003. Things have now improved in China and most new flat and house dwellers can adjust and control their heating and AC at will.

4. Things have now changed and couples can have more than one child.

5. Tiananmen Square is in the centre of Beijing, and it means "Gate of Heavenly Peace". It is one of the largest squares in the world. Many important historical and cultural events have taken place there, including the infamous massacre in 1989. It has a huge portrait of Mao Zedong overlooking it.

CHAPTER SEVEN - US

1. Trucks are used by workmen in the UK for jobs, and are not in regular use. I was rather taken aback that my future husband came to meet his bride-to-be in such a contraption.

2. Wadi is an Arabic word meaning a valley, ravine or a channel that's dry except in the rainy season. It is used in English parlance and it means a dry river bed.

CHAPTER EIGHT - An Innocent Abroad

1. A luminaria or farolito is a small paper brown bag, weighed down with some sand and a candle placed in the middle. These paper lanterns are popular in New Mexico at Christmastime. They are also widely used in Hispanic culture.

2. *Linen 'n Things* went out of business a few years later.

3. An adobe brick is a mud brick mixed with straw. In New Mexico many old houses were built with these mud bricks. Adobe homes are cool in the summer and warm in winter. Each adobe brick weighs around 40lbs.

4. Glyndebourne is an English country house, the site of an opera house that, since 1934, has been the venue for the annual Glyndebourne

Opera Festival. Initially, operas were presented within the house but there is now a free-standing opera house in its grounds. It forms part of the English "season" which includes the Royal Ascot horse races, Henley Regatta, and Wimbledon tennis championships. The Santa Fe Opera season in New Mexico is also held in the summer and is world-famous.

5. Chicano or Chicana, is a chosen identity of some Mexican Americans in the United States. Chicano or Xicano are sometimes used interchangeably with Mexican-American, and both names exist as chosen identities within the Mexican-American community in the United States. This differentiates them from recent Mexican immigrants.

www.ingramcontent.com/pod-product-compliance
Lightning Source LLC
Chambersburg PA
CBHW071731120626
46550CB00002B/472